5 conversations you **must** have with **your** daughter

THE BIBLE STUDY

Vicki Courtney

LifeWay Press®
Nashville, Tennessee

ISBN: 1415867348
Item: 005191375

This book is a resource for course CG-1439 in the Personal
Life category of the Christian Growth Study Plan.

Dewey Decimal Classification: 248.843
Subject Headings:WOMEN \ MOTHERS AND DAUGHTERS \ SPIRITUAL LIFE

To order additional copies of this resource, write to LifeWay Church Resources Customer
Service, One LifeWay Plaza, Nashville TN 37234-0113; fax (615) 251-5933; phone toll free
(800) 458-2772; order online at *www.lifeway.com;* e-mail *orderentry@lifeway.com;* or visit the
LifeWay Christian Store serving you.

Printed in the United States of America

Leadership and Adult Publishing
LifeWay Church Resources
One LifeWay Plaza
Nashville, TN 37234-0175

CONTENTS

ABOUT THIS STUDY

This six-session Bible study, for moms of daughters from the cradle to college, is built around five conversations that should be ongoing in girls' formative years:

Conversation 1: You are more than the sum of your parts.
Conversation 2: Don't be in such a hurry to grow up.
Conversation 3: Sex is great and worth the wait.
Conversation 4: It's OK to dream about marriage and motherhood.
Conversation 5: Girls gone wild are a dime a dozen—dare to be virtuous.

5 Conversations The Bible Study gives moms practical advice on how to talk with their daughters about sensitive issues in a godly way—and provides them personal encouragement and support along the way.

Six group sessions engage moms in learning from each other; hearing from Vicki and discussing issues and truths she raises; and discerning how God would direct them in their parenting journey.

Each group session introduces the concepts moms will interact with during the week. Session 1 is both an introduction to the study and a launch to conversation 1; sessions 2-5 set the context for the corresponding conversations; and session 6 is a concluding challenge to keep those conversations going!

Home features, reading much like magazine articles, can take as little as 15-20 minutes a day or more as desired. Moms can read all at once or one a day. These elements are a part of the workbook:

- **Let's Talk** introduces new concepts.
- **Personal Reflection** features ask a mom to consider her stance on an issue.
- **God's Take on the Issue** reveals what the Bible has to say about a subject.
- **Conversation Starters** are optional questions on each video guide for your group to unpack further as desired.

- **Conversation Boosters** give a mother practical ideas (and some practice) on how to start important discussions with her daughter. Age-appropriate suggestions are periodically given for moms with girls ages 5 and under, ages 6-10, ages 11-14, and ages 15-18.
- **Bringing It Home** helps moms apply concepts to daily life.
- **Frequent use of statistics, trends, and research** expose cultural lies for moms and daughters seeking God's ways in a culture that often leads otherwise.

Suggestions for the facilitator of a 5 Conversations group, on pages 169-174 of this book, assume 75- to 90-minute sessions.

In addition, a leader kit (item 005125844) is available, with one copy of the member book and two DVDs. Teaching sessions are on DVD 1, and Meet Our Moms bonus footage is on DVD 2.

The bonus footage features the moms in Vicki's video small group: Melissa, Melanie, Chris, and Karen. Each mother-daughter relationship represents different ages and stages, and your group may resonate with the stories these moms have. The bonus footage also may be used to promote your study, to consider different responses to a conversation, or to further enrich your study. Periodically check *www.lifeway.com/5conversations* for how other moms are doing this study.

Decide whether to meet in homes or in a church setting. In either setting, make sure the space is inviting for the group. Discuss with your pastor or church staff how to provide member books for each participant; you may need to collect payment during session 1. Art elements from this book, on *www.lifeway.com/5conversations*, can be used for name tags and other items.

Be sure to register participants as they come to your first meeting, especially if outreach is a goal.

Vicki opens and closes her video with this affirmation:

> *God is looking for imperfect mothers raising imperfect daughters in an imperfect world—who are desperately dependent on a perfect God for the results.*

This statement expresses the desired goal and outcome of this Bible study.

ABOUT THE AUTHOR

Vicki Courtney is a sought-after speaker and best-selling author with a ministry that reaches more than 150,000 girls and mothers each year. A mother herself, of three children, she seeks to provide tweens, teens, and their parents with the tools necessary to navigate today's promiscuous culture. Vicki's popular blog, VirtueAlert.com, receives a quarter of a million visitors annually.

With hundreds of radio and newspaper interviews to her credit, Vicki has also appeared on CNN, Fox News, and CNN Headline News as a youth culture commentator to address various issues impacting tweens and teens. Creator of VirtuousReality.com, this online magazine for teen girls has attracted visitors from all 50 states and more than 30 countries.

She is author of numerous books, including *Your Girl: Raising a Godly Daughter in an Ungodly World* and its counterpart, *Your Boy: Raising a Godly Son in an Ungodly World*; *Logged On and Tuned Out*; and *5 Conversations You Must Have With Your Daughter*. A two-time ECPA Christian Book Award winner, Vicki has authored a series of magazine-style books for both tween girls (*Between*) and teen girls (*TeenVirtue*).

In addition to this 5 Conversations Bible study, Vicki is author of popular Bible studies for women including *The Virtuous Woman* and *Get A Life!*, plus the DVD Bible study for teen girls, *His Girl*, and the DVD Bible study for moms, *Your Girl*.

Vicki resides in Austin, Texas, with her husband, Keith, and three children. In her spare time, she enjoys Starbucks® Grande Vanilla Lattes, shoe shopping, and spending time with her family. You can visit Vicki at *www.VickiCourtney.com*.

Bethany McShurley, leader guide writer, is a freelance editor/writer who specializes in Christian curriculum and new author development. She hopes to spread the message that a relationship with Jesus can radically transform every aspect of life. Bethany resides in Maryland with her husband, Jon, and two sons.

INTRO AND CONVERSATION 1

You Are More than the Sum of Your Parts

God is looking for imperfect mothers raising imperfect daughters in an imperfect world who are desperately dependent on a perfect God for the results.

1. Teach our daughters _____ ____ _____ _____.

1 Timothy 4:8: *For physical training is of some value, but _____ has value for all things, holding promise for both the present life and the life to come.*

1 Samuel 16:7: *"Man looks at the outward appearance, but the LORD looks at the _____ ."*

2. Take a closer look at _____ .

What was the _____ you received from your mom or dad?

Let your daughter know you are a _____ ____ _____ .

Ask God to _____ your heart to take thoughts captive.

CONVERSATION STARTERS with your group:
- Have you ever judged someone or shown favor based on appearance? If so, what were the circumstances?
- Vicki talks about a shift from virtue to vanity. If you agree a shift has occurred, when and why do you think it happened?

Weekly challenge:

Interested in reviewing this or other 5 Conversations Bible study sessions? You can download all digital sessions by going to www.lifeway.com/women.

VIDEO GUIDE

SESSION1

WEEK 1
Redefining Beauty

Emily Dickinson
~

"Beauty is not caused. It is."

PRETTY PACKAGING

let's talk I'm a sucker for pretty
packaging. Every year our Sunday School class has
an annual Christmas party complete with a gift
exchange, and every year, without fail, I pick the
prettiest wrapped present under the tree. You'd think
I'd learn my lesson after coming home year after year
with such noteworthy luxuries as matching his-and-
hers reindeer-head slippers and a plastic foot attached
to a trouser leg to hang out the trunk of my car. (And
no, I didn't use either one—well, except maybe the
slippers. Once.) Clearly, when it comes to a
pretty package, what you see is not always
what you get.

"I've never seen
a smiling face
that was not
beautiful."
Author Unknown

"The proportion
of her face is
beautiful. She's
a great package,
beautifully put
together."
Director Oliver Stone

Describe a time when you fell prey to pretty
packaging and ended up disappointed with
the contents inside.

Product manufacturers who aim for successful sales
know the importance of packaging. Further, they know
that consumers make as many as 70 percent of their buying

decisions in the store and can face up to 100,000 items that bid for their atten-tion.[1] Whether it's a pack of gum, a tube of toothpaste, or a bag of chips, you can bet that countless dollars and hours have been invested into analyzing everything from that item's target audience to color palettes and shelf placement. The end goal, of course, is for the product to stand out on the shelf and, above all, to get picked up by the consumer and scanned at the checkout.

Now, what if I told you that your daughter is also a product? Her "brand managers" work around the clock to make sure she knows exactly what it takes to get noticed. If she is to catch the eye of her target audience, the packaging must be perfect. And by perfect, I mean *flawless*.

> **What are some messages girls today receive regarding their outward appearance?**

By the time your daughter celebrates her twelfth birthday, she will have seen an estimated 77,546 commercials.[2] Add to that the images she sees daily from maga-zines, billboards, and the Internet, and you can be certain that by the time she blows out 16 candles, she will have a mental checklist of what it takes to achieve the world's brand of beauty. Over and over again she will be told to lose weight, tone up, dress provocatively, and "flaunt it."

It shouldn't come as a surprise that 58 percent of girls describe themselves in negative terms, including words such as *disgusting* and *ugly*. Nearly 4 out of 10 engage in unhealthy eating behaviors, such as anorexia or bulimia.[3] The sad truth is, most young women report feeling anxious and stressed about some aspect of their looks when getting ready for the day.

PERSONAL reflection

Rate below the level of anxiety or stress you face about aspects of your appearance.

Low	Moderate	High

Which of the following issues cause you the most concern?

- Weight
- Clothes that feel too tight
- Lack of muscle tone
- Tooth discoloration/dental needs
- Lack of "fashion sense"
- Varicose veins or sunspots
- Outdated wardrobe

- Cellulite
- Complexion
- Facial wrinkles
- Haircut/color
- Body shape
- Chest size
- Other

Which of these issues might also concern your daughter? Don't assume she has to be a certain age to worry about such things.

GOD'S TAKE on the issue

When Samuel was called by God to anoint the king to follow Saul, God taught the prophet a valuable lesson.

Read 1 Samuel 16:6-7. Why did Samuel initially think Eliab was next in line for the throne (v. 6)?
- Eliab presented Samuel with two letters of recommendation and won him over with his king-like charm.
- Samuel took one look at Eliab's height and handsome features and thought, *Wow, this kid has "king" written all over him.*
- Eliab's senior class voted him "Most Likely to be King of Israel."

Samuel's first impression of Eliab was based on looks. The truth is, we all share the tendency to do the same in our interactions with people. A shapely model says "This is the car to buy" and we believe her. A handsome man gives us a compliment and we assign it more worth than we would give the same words coming from someone less appealing.

At what did God specifically tell Samuel not to look (v. 7a)?

By what standard does God judge beauty (v. 7)?

 PERSONAL reflection

As a person "thinks in his heart, so is he" (Prov. 23:7, NKJV). Just as your heart sends life-giving blood to your body, so does the word *heart* describe the starting place of our thoughts, beliefs, values, motives, and convictions.

In the past 30 days, have you felt anxiety or stress about aspects of your heart?　　● Yes　● No

If yes, list some of your concerns.

Overall, do you spend more time focusing on ways to improve your heart or on ways to improve your appearance?

What about your daughter? On what does she focus?

How has God spoken to your heart today?

DAY 2

THE SIZE DEMISE AND THE WEIGHT DEBATE

let's talk

On a recent afternoon while shopping with my daughter, I waited outside a dressing room while she tried on some jeans. In the dressing room next to her, a young lady yelled to her friend, "I am so fat! I can't fit into these size zero's. Will you go get me a size two?" Seriously, I wanted to crawl under the door of that dressing room and feed the girl a cheeseburger. I prayed my daughter had ignored the entire exchange, but chances are it became yet another chink in the armor of the body-image battle that wages war within the souls of most women, young and old alike. Rather than logically deducing that statements like this are the product of the culture's narrow definition of beauty, most girls within hearing range will glance at themselves in the mirror and feel disgust and shame. Some will respond by binging and purging. Others will starve themselves. Still others will seek temporary solace by overeating.

But most, I dare say, will suffer in silence. By age 13, 53 percent of American girls will be unhappy with their bodies and by age 17, an estimated 78 percent will be dissatisfied.[4]

PERSONAL reflection

At what age do you recall first experiencing dissatisfaction with your body? Describe the circumstances.

In what ways do those feelings continue to haunt you?

Does your daughter know about any negative feelings you have about your shape? ● Yes ● No ● I'm not sure

Did you know that the garment industry designs clothing to fit the hourglass shape? Yet ironically, a study found that the hourglass figure is the least dominant shape of women, having made up only 8 percent of the women in the study. The study further found that the hourglass shape almost does not exist in women larger than a size eight.[5] Now, keep in mind that the average woman is 5' 3.8" and weighs 163 pounds.[6] Because of this misconception, many women are unable to find clothes designed to flatter their body shape and, as a result, they struggle to make peace with their God-given bodies. In fact, 46 percent of women were found to have more of a rectangle shape, 21 percent were spoon shaped, and 14 percent were shaped more like an inverted triangle.[7]

Given the information in the last paragraph, what percent of women are trying to fit their non-hourglass shape into clothes designed to fit the industry's hourglass standard? Circle your answer.

32%   52%   92%

How does that make you feel?

I recently asked preteen girls (ages 8-12), "What's your one worry when it comes to your body shape?" Their responses include the following:

That when my chest develops, it will draw attention. *(Taylor, age 11)*
Getting fat. I always want to stay fit—it really worries me. *(Keagan, 10)*
Being the last one to develop. *(Elise, 12)*
I'm really skinny and not curvy. *(Bethany, 12)*
Not being tall or having big enough boobs. *(Kaelan, 10)*
That I won't develop in certain places. *(Breanna, 12)*
Not being tall enough. *(Sarah, 10)*
That I'll be too tall. *(Morgan, 11)*

Read Psalm 139:14.

 ## PERSONAL reflection

What are you doing or what can you do to raise your girl(s) to help them know "full well" that they are "fearfully and wonderfully made" and, in turn, can praise God that His works are wonderful?

Do you accept that you too are fearfully and wonderfully made?

What behaviors or actions do you think might prove that a woman knows "that full well"?

Now, don't misunderstand me: I am certainly not saying that Psalm 139:14 gives justification for over- or under-eating and poor exercise habits. I'm all about temple maintenance. The way I see it, God wants us to take care of the temple, but there is a wide variation when it comes to what constitutes a "healthy temple."

Somehow we as Christians have allowed the culture to develop a blueprint for what the temple should look like.

Be honest. Which of the following is emphasized more in your home?
- Looking like a super model: Staying in a narrow target weight range and exercising to stay toned.
- General exercise and nutrition: Staying in a reasonable weight range with good health being the overall goal.
- Little Debbie™ is our personal trainer: The pantry is open 24 hours a day and it's a regular snackfest free-for-all.

According to scriptural principles the goal should be health and nutrition rather than size and weight. God has more to say on this matter.

GOD'S TAKE on the issue

Read 1 Timothy 4:8 and describe God's attitude on physical exercise.

Which is more important to you—that you stay in good physical or spiritual shape?
- Physical
- Spiritual
- Both
- Neither
- The answer varies depending on the day!

Which of the following "spiritual exercises" do you currently model to your daughter? Check or circle all that apply.

- Daily Bible reading
- An active prayer life
- Tithing/giving to mission causes
- Local church involvement
- Bible study participation
- Worship as an attitude of the heart
- Concern for the lost
- Discipleship (of your daughter)

I don't want to oversimplify the solution, and I certainly don't claim to be a nutrition expert. In fact, my children were fed far too much junk food, and were it not for the fact that we are a small-boned family with a high metabolism, we'd all be in a heap of trouble. I am just as attached to my grande vanilla lattes and cookies-and-cream ice cream as the next girl. I too am learning as I go and am working to improve in this area of health and nutrition. Always a work in progress, huh?

Today's lesson may be painful for some of you. Will you take that pain and lay it at the throne of God? Will you allow Him to comfort any past insecurities or hurts? Remember, you can't pass down a healthy attitude regarding body image unless you first own it for yourself.

BRINGING IT home

Consider the following tips to help your daughter develop a positive body image. Choose to start putting at least one into practice this week.

1. Give your daughter positive messages that she is beautiful.

In *Teenage Girls: Exploring Issues Adolescent Girls Face and Strategies to Help Them*, author Ginny Olson states that "mothers especially have a clear impact on their daughter's body image. Girls who have strong and healthy relationships with their mothers are more likely to have a higher sense of self-confidence and a lower incidence of eating disorders."[8] Tell your daughter what you like about her physical looks. Things like her good posture, overall poise, and grace do count!

2. Mothers, watch what you say about your own bodies.

Darlene Atkins, the director of the Eating Disorders Clinic at Children's National Medical Center in Washington states, "Sadly, mothers especially are often very critical of their own weight and shape, and their girls absorb that."[9] Don't allow negativity about your perceived shortcomings to meet your daughter's ears.

3. Make nutrition rather than weight loss the focus in your home.

In the article "For teens, obesity no laughing matter," Darlene Atkins advocated making home a "safe zone," primarily by emphasizing feeding one's body in a healthy way so that it functions at a healthy level—not by dwelling on restrictive dieting. To further support the need to back up talk with action, Kay Abrams, a clinical psychologist and eating disorders expert, says, "Live by your actions and your lifestyle. Don't lecture and talk about weight all the time. Just change."[10]

Don't pick up another box of snack cakes at the grocery store. Stock up on peanut butter and celery, low fat cheese, and fresh berries. Make eating healthful foods fun.

4. Never make teasing remarks about your daughter's weight.

According to research from the University of Minnesota, teasing adolescents about weight—especially if it comes from family members—can play a big role in future weight problems. The study found that girls who were teased about their weight were about twice as likely to be overweight five years later as girls who were not. In addition, they were also about 1.5 times more likely to engage in binge eating and use extreme weight-control behaviors, such as purging or abuse of laxatives.

Even more disturbing, the study found that almost half of the overweight girls she surveyed were teased by their families, compared to 34 percent of overweight boys. Note that this is not teasing as in harassment but rather simple statements made tongue-in-cheek: "Are you sure you should eat that?" or "Whoa there! That milkshake will go straight to your thighs!"[11] The next time a weight-related wise-crack pops into your mind, replace it with a verbal assurance of your love.

BEAUTY BY HOLLYWOOD

let's talk

When Mariah Carey appeared on "American Idol" as guest mentor, a backstage diva episode occurred during a photo shoot for the show. As FoxNews.com reported, she showed up in a tight-fitting outfit, but the shoot took longer than expected. One insider disclosed, "Tech and camera guys were made to put in extra effort putting up lights and having them angled perfectly, with Carey's people 'double checking' that she was positioned perfectly at all times." 'We had to reshoot [her response to] one of the questions,' … change the lighting and alter the position and do it again because we went off angle slightly. She has a director of photography with her at all times and can only be shot from the waist up.'"[12]

The average woman is 5 feet 3.8 inches and weighs 163 pounds. The average teen girl is 5 feet 3.8 inches and 134.5 pounds. The average runway model is 5 feet 11 inches and 120 pounds.

According to a study of middle school girls, physical perfection means a height of 5 feet 7 inches and a weight of 110 pounds.

Seriously, gag me. When I read about Mariah's diva fit, Ecclesiastes 1:2 came to mind: "Vanity of vanities, saith the Preacher, vanity of vanities; all is vanity" (KJV). A study commissioned by The Dove Foundation (an organization committed to wholesome family entertainment) found that 57 percent of all women strongly agree that "the attributes of female beauty have become very narrowly defined in today's world," and 68 percent strongly agree that "the media and advertising set an unrealistic standard of beauty that most women can't ever achieve."[13]

PERSONAL reflection

Which best describes your response to airbrushed images of perfect celebrity bodies? Check all that apply.

- Even though I know Hollywood images are doctored, they still leave me with the feeling that I can never measure up. Sometimes I feel a little ashamed of my "flaws."
- I am angry that normal body shapes and sizes are not used in ads. How many people really wear a size 2 and never have a pimple?
- I feel pity for the emaciated models. When I see them, I have a strong desire to feed them a dozen glazed donuts.
- I try to remain thankful for the skin I'm in and to remember that God sees me as "fearfully and wonderfully made" (Ps. 139:14).
- I avoid airbrushed images as much as possible. Those perfect-looking bodies depress me, so I stay away.

Do you think it's possible to shield your daughter from airbrushed and/or surgically enhanced images of celebrities?

- No   - Yes   - Maybe

I don't want to depress you, but the answer to the final question is no. We can limit our daughters' exposure to the fantasy faces and forms Hollywood declares beautiful, but we can't safeguard them from exposure 100 percent of the time. Therefore, our only choice is to teach our daughters early on to discern the images they are exposed to in an effort to identify and break down the lies of the culture.

GOD'S TAKE on the issue

Romans 12:2 represents the tug-of-war our daughters face as they are exposed to the culture's influence regarding beauty and the female body.

Write Romans 12:2 in the margin using your preferred Bible translation.

How can you avoid conforming to the world's way of thinking?

What do you think it means to "be transformed by the renewing of your mind" (KJV and NIV)?

The New Living Translation describes "renewal of the mind" as "changing the way you think." When we change the way we think about beauty, our attitude toward it and toward ourselves is transformed. The flip side is that when we don't allow God to renew our minds through what He has to say about a topic, we leave ourselves open to any message culture throws our way. This is particularly scary in the case of young girls.

In the book *Teenage Girls: Exploring Issues Adolescent Girls Face and Strategies to Help Them*, author Ginny Olson states:

"Early adolescent girls are especially vulnerable to media images. They're constantly searching for information to guide them as to how they should look and behave. … As concrete thinkers, they haven't yet developed the necessary skills for discerning the different messages the media is sending. It's not until they reach about middle adolescence that they begin to develop the ability to scrutinize media messages and evaluate the themes with a certain level of skepticism. By the time they reach 17 or 18, they've had enough experience with the media to be able to assess and reject the messages."[14]

To what media messages is your daughter exposed that could leave her with unrealistic expectations regarding her body image?

What can you do to help her form realistic expectations instead?

Note that if your daughter is younger than 17, she has not yet gained full cognitive ability to scrutinize media messages. That's where we come in. Even though we can't avoid exposure to negative media messages 100 percent of the time, we can offer damage control when they occur. We must offer our girls assistance in breaking the media messages down into a language they will understand.

Mothers, if we want our daughters to "know what God wants them to do" and thus tap into the treasure of His "good, pleasing and perfect will" (NIV), we must help them break down these messages until they gain the spiritual maturity to do so on their own. Part of our job is to help our girls filter the misinformation culture sends them by reminding them of the facts—for which we don't need to look any further than God's Word.

CONVERSATION boosters

I want to end by giving you several age-appropriate scenarios you may encounter with your daughter. Choose the one that matches your daughter's age and script a sample conversation in the space. You could have a conversation with her that would both disarm media lies and teach her godly truth. Try it! Getting started is the first step.

If your daughter is under age 5:

You are at the grocery store checkout. Your daughter notices a model with a seemingly perfect, but no doubt airbrushed, body on a magazine cover. She makes a comment about how "pretty" the lady is.

You say:

If your daughter is 6-10:

Your daughter has a friend over and you make them cookies. You leave the room and overhear the friend saying, "I don't want to eat too many cookies or my mom said I will get fat." Later that evening you take the opportunity to talk to your daughter.

You say:

If your daughter is 11-14:

Your daughter has a girlfriend over to spend the night. When you go upstairs to check on them, they are perusing several fashion magazines her friend has brought. You kindly tell them to find something else to do, but after the friend leaves, you talk to your daughter.

You say:

If your daughter is 15-18:

Your daughter is on the cheer squad and it is uniform fitting day. Several of the girls comment on cellulite they have on their legs. One says, "I'll die if I can't get rid of this before I wear this skirt." Later you take the opportunity to talk to your daughter.

You say:

FALLOUT FROM THE SEXY CRAZE

let's talk **While attending one of my daughter's cheer competitions several years ago, I had one of those heart-stopping moments. No, she didn't trip up in a tumbling pass. "It" happened during an intermission while the judges tabulated scores. The announcer called all the girls to gather in the middle of the floor to pass the time with a little fun. "The Macarena" began to play on the loudspeakers and the gym mat became an instant sea of girls from age 6 to 18 dancing and singing to the catchy song. There were plenty of *ooh's* and *aah's* as parents watched their little ones trying to imitate the older girls: "One, little two, little three, Macarena; four, little five, little six, Macarena." And then the jaw-dropping moment occurred. The announcer, a fellow mom, chimed in: "C'mon girls, work it! You can do better than that! Be SEXY!"**

"Just because I look sexy on the cover of *Rolling Stone* doesn't mean I'm naughty."

Britney Spears

Excuse me? Did she just tell a room full of impressionable girls to be sexy? Without a word to my friends sitting beside me, I got up and made my way to the registration table, where I lodged a formal complaint. I was offended and my daughter was 14! Little girls shouldn't be exposed to the word *sexy*, much less told to act that way!

If ever a topic makes my blood boil, it's the rampant sexualization of our girls. What's with our culture's obsession over turning our girls, both young and old, into sexpots? Check out these real-life examples of slogans that have been found on apparel items for girls:

"Made to tease kitten"

"Teeze me"

"Hooters girl (in training)"

Peekaboo pole dancing kit for girls includes a sexy garter to "unleash the sex kitten inside" and "earn Peekaboo Dance Dollars"

"Wink, wink" and "Eye candy": This slogan was actually found on, believe it or not, thong underwear for girls 7-14!

> **How do you feel after reading these examples of sexualization? Check the ones that apply.**
> - **No big deal. If it offends someone, she shouldn't buy the product.**
> - **It makes me mad, but you can't fight every battle.**
> - **Where's the nearest Amish community? There's something to be said for those plain dresses.**

Chances are you remember the rumblings in the news about the ground-breaking discovery by the American Psychological Association that the proliferation of sexualized images of girls and young women in advertising, merchandising, and media is harmful to girls' self-image and healthy development.[15] Sexualization was defined by the task force as occurring when a person's value comes only from her/his sexual appeal or behavior, to the exclusion of other characteristics, and when a person is sexually objectified: made into a thing for another's sexual use.

While the overall finding of the study may not come as a surprise, it should serve as a wake-up call for parents who somehow rationalize this is not a battle worth fighting. Take a look at some of the fallout the study confirmed.

Cognitive and Emotional Consequences

Sexualization and objectification undermine a person's confidence in and comfort with her own body, leading to emotional and self-image problems such as shame and anxiety.

Mental and Physical Health

Research links sexualization with three of the most common mental health problems diagnosed in girls and women—eating disorders, low self-esteem, and depression or depressed mood.

Sexual Development

Research suggests that the sexualization of girls has negative consequences on girls' ability to develop a healthy sexual self-image.[16]

GOD'S TAKE on the issue

Read 1 Timothy 2:9. Why do you think God felt it important to include this verse in His inspired Word?

How does our fashion culture regard adherence to modesty and discretion?

How do you think that conflicts with God's desire for women?

According to the APA study, parents may actually contribute to the sexualization of their daughters in a number of ways. One way is to convey the message that maintaining an attractive physical appearance is the most important goal for girls.

PERSONAL reflection

When taking an honest appraisal, do you think you or your husband place too much emphasis on physical appearance for either yourself or for your daughter? If so, give an example.

If outer appearance is out of balance to you, chances are you have passed the same mind-set on to your daughter. Hopefully after reading this section you will have a better grasp on why God tells us that we are "fearfully and wonderfully made" and further wants us to "know that full well" (Ps. 139:14). It may even be necessary to go to your daughter and apologize for any part you have played in emphasizing outer appearance to an unhealthy degree. There have certainly been times when I have had to own up to this with my own daughter.

If you have been minimizing the immodest fashion craze, you will be interested in what the APA study had to say in this regard:

> If girls purchase (or ask parents to purchase) products and clothes designed to make them look physically appealing and sexy, and if they style their identities after the sexy celebrities who populate their cultural landscape, they are, in effect, sexualizing themselves. Girls also sexualize themselves when they think of themselves in objectified terms. Psychological researchers have identified self-objectification as a key process whereby girls learn to think of and treat their bodies as objects of others' desires. In self-objectification, girls internalize an observer's perspective on their physical selves and learn to treat themselves as objects to be looked at and evaluated for their appearance.[17]

In what ways could parents play a role in their daughter's "self-objectification"? In your opinion, what might cause a parent to do so?

Many girls are not yet able to make a connection between what they wear and the reaction it may generate among the opposite sex. The APA study found that girls are experiencing teen pressures at younger ages. However, they are not able to deal with these issues because their cognitive development is out of sync with their social, emotional, and sexual development. Let girls be girls.

In *For Young Women Only* Shaunti Feldhahn cites the results of a survey in which guys were asked questions pertaining to the way girls dress. The study found that when girls dress in such a way as to call attention to their bodies, 85 percent of guys said they would have a temptation to picture her naked (then or later). The survey further confirmed that the majority of guys thought she was dressing that way because she wanted them to picture her that way. Feldhahn's survey of girls found that in reality only less than 4 percent of girls dress in a revealing fashion in an attempt to get guys to fantasize about them.[18]

Which best describes your response to these survey results?
- These guys should be ashamed of themselves!
- No surprise; isn't attracting the attention of the opposite sex what fashion is all about?
- I'm never letting my daughter out of the house again.
- I never thought about it that way, but it makes me sad.

It is up to us to have this conversation about sexuality and modesty over and over again with our daughters. We've got to remind them that clothing sends a strong message and may, in fact, be a message that misrepresents who they really are. When it comes to sporting the perfect outfit, we need to let our daughters know that there is nothing wrong with dressing fashionably as long as it meets God's standard of dress—modestly, with decency and propriety.

BRINGING IT home

What steps can you take to provide a protective guard between your daughter and the rampant sexualization of girls today?

PRETTY IS AS PRETTY DOES

While thumbing through a *People* **magazine's "Most Beautiful People" edition, I read a tribute to a Hollywood actress who is known far and wide for her physical beauty. She is also known for philanthropy to third-world countries and has three adopted children from some of the countries where she participated in volunteer relief missions. Her resume boasts a title few can claim: United Nations goodwill ambassador.**

"Pretty is something you're born with. But beautiful, that's an equal opportunity adjective."

Author Unknown

"Beauty is in the eye of the beholder and it may be necessary from time to time to give a stupid or misinformed beholder a black eye."

Miss Piggy

People magazine crowned her "2006 Most Beautiful Star" and ran the following byline to the announcement: Find out how Hollywood's most dedicated humanitarian stays gorgeous inside and out. (No makeup required!) I think most would agree that this woman sounds like a beautiful person. But what if I told you this same woman fell in love with a married man (a fellow actor) and had a rumored affair? Her lover subsequently divorced his wife to be with her and the two have lived together since. They have six children, all out of wedlock, and appear in no hurry to tie the knot.

Proverbs 11:22 says, "Like a gold ring in a pig's snout is a beautiful woman who shows no discretion." By biblical standards, this admired actress fails to make the "Most Beautiful" list. Unfortunately, our daughters will be consistently exposed to the culture's cheap imitation of beauty and, in turn, many will be desensitized to God's standard. With a heavy emphasis on physical appearance, the label of "beautiful" will be saved for an elite minority—unless we as moms step in and become proactive in redefining beauty.

> The Dove Campaign asked women in a large survey if they would describe themselves as "beautiful." Guess how many considered themselves beautiful? Circle your answer.
>
> 14%   8%   2%

Believe it or not, only 2 percent of women claimed they would describe themselves as beautiful. Would you be one of them? What about your daughter? So what exactly is beauty? The Dove Campaign asked women about beauty and found that:

- Seventy-seven percent strongly agree that beauty can be achieved through attitude, spirit, and other attributes that have nothing to do with physical appearance.
- Eighty-nine percent strongly agree that a woman can be beautiful at any age.
- Eighty-five percent state that every woman has something about her that is beautiful.[19]

Interestingly, the study found that two-thirds of women strongly agree that physical attractiveness is about how one looks whereas beauty includes more of who a person is. Women rate happiness, confidence, dignity, and humor as powerful components of beauty, along with the more traditional attributes of physical appearance, body weight and shape, and even a sense of style.[20]

PERSONAL reflection

When you hear (or say) the phrase, "She is beautiful," is it generally made in reference to what is on the outside or what is on the inside?

What about when you say "She is beautiful"?

What about when your daughter says it?

GOD'S TAKE on the issue

I find it sad that popular culture and mass media have hijacked the authentic definition of beauty. Beauty is defined by God and God alone. He sets the standard for beauty and gives us clues throughout Scripture as to what defines a beautiful woman. Amazingly, one passage of Scripture supports the women in the Dove survey who rate happiness, confidence, dignity, and humor as powerful components of beauty.

> Read Proverbs 31:10-31. List key phrases in the passage that describe qualities of inner beauty.

> Proverbs 31:30 sheds light on the best beauty secret on the market. What is it?

> What do you think it means to "fear the Lord"?

Awe and reverence of a loving and forgiving God are the foundation of all manifestations of beauty. Physical beauty fades over time, but true beauty (virtue) is timeless. That's why it's important we place more emphasis on a healthy heart (spiritually speaking) than on physical appearance.

Would you say that the pursuit of virtue is a priority in your life?

How have you emphasized this priority to your daughter?

As you think about God's standard of beauty, list five women you know who are truly beautiful. Alongside each name note qualities that make her beautiful.

1.

2.

3.

4.

5.

Have you pointed out any of these women to your daughter as "beautiful women"?

We must faithfully remind our daughters that beauty is not defined by a number on a scale, a pre-manufactured clothing size, an hourglass shape, pouty lips, designer low-rise jeans, a sassy haircut, a clear complexion, an anti-wrinkle cream, or a surgical procedure. While some of the above may garner catcalls from men, they don't impress God in the least.

BRINGING IT home

First Peter 3:3-4 tells us, "Your adornment must not be merely external—braiding the hair, and wearing gold jewelry, or putting on dresses; but let it be the hidden person of the heart, with the imperishable quality of a gentle and quiet spirit, which is precious in the sight of God" (NASB).

Write a note to your daughter and put this passage of Scripture into your own words.

Use this space for practice; then copy it onto some pretty stationery. Consider telling her about some of the struggles you have had when it comes to rejecting the world's narrow definition of beauty and accepting God's standard. If she is too young to understand your note, save it for when she is older.

Talk a minute to thank God for His standard of beauty. Ask Him to help you in the effort to redefine beauty and point your daughter to His perfect standard. Then find the scenario that most closely resembles your daughter's life stage. Use the suggestions to help your daughter form a godly definition of beauty and to deepen her sense of self worth.

If your daughter is 5 years or younger:

Chances are, you remember hearing, "What a beautiful baby," when your daughter was an infant. And chances are, you have said it countless times to others.

While our infants are unable to absorb the message, it won't be long before they can. Be careful to find a healthy balance when it comes to complimenting your daughter's appearance. On the one hand, our girls naturally want to be told they are pretty. If we don't tell them, it could leave them craving male attention in the years ahead. On the other hand, we don't want to go overboard and send a message that worth is based on what they look like. This could set them up for disappointment when compliments diminish. Strike a balance by saving the word *beautiful* to describe those who possess true attributes of virtue.

If your daughter is 6-11 years:

As your daughter moves through grade school, she will begin to absorb the culture's message regarding beauty. Whether she is being influenced primarily by the media or her friends, one thing is for certain: She is hearing a buzz about what constitutes beauty in the world's eyes. It will be especially important to have open communication with your daughter regarding these messages.

Take advantage of teachable moments, whether they are ads you come across or a friend's comments. Remind her of God's standard of beauty as it is detailed in 1 Samuel 16:17; 1 Peter 3:3-4; and Proverbs 31:10-31.

If your daughter seems overly attentive to appearance and body-image issues, try to find out where the influence is coming from. Is it from a friend? Is she exposed to media messages that she is too young to process? (For example, is she allowed to watch PG-13 movies, view TV shows, or listen to music that supports a narrow, unrealistic definition of beauty?) Could you or your husband be focusing too much on appearance and sending her the wrong message?

Again, emphasize qualities of virtue over appearance. The message should always be temple maintenance: healthy weight range, good eating habits, exercise, positive grooming habits. As she moves into latter years of elementary school, begin necessary conversations about the process her body (and her friends' bodies) will go through as they move from girlhood to womanhood.

If your daughter is 12 years or older:

When I surveyed adult Christian women, one of the questions I asked was: "What sort of message did you receive from your mom/dad regarding weight and body image when you were growing up?" Many women shared that even today they could still remember exact phrases and the sting they felt over comments made by their parents during middle and high school years.

Even if your daughter needs to lose weight, it's best if the pediatrician breaks the news rather than parents' constantly "nagging" about the matter. And for the record, if the pediatrician isn't worried, you shouldn't be either. Again, a better approach is to emphasize nutrition, exercise, and hygiene and lead by example. Practice it; don't preach it.

Make certain that your comments are scarce related to your daughter's (and others') appearance, weight, and body shape. If you are preoccupied with these things, chances are, your daughter will be too. Allow her to hear you compliment women who are truly worthy of being labeled beautiful—those who are virtuous.

CONVERSATION 2

Don't Be in Such a Hurry to Grow Up

At one time society and moms were on the _____ _____.

Be more of a _____ than a provoker.

Don't just throw your daughter into the world
without any _____. _____ _____.

We have every right as parents to draw some _____
_____. We don't have to say no to everything.

SESSION2

CONVERSATION STARTERS with your group:

- In what ways are you helping your girl maintain her girlhood?
- Share some ways you have learned to balance saying *yes*, *no*, and *wait* on some growing-up issues. (Or share one of our mom's responses to this question, from DVD 2.)
- How has your daughter caught you off guard recently? How did you respond?

Weekly challenge:

*Interested in reviewing this or other 5 Conversations Bible study sessions?
You can download all digital sessions by going to www.lifeway.com/women.*

37

WEEK 2
Reclaiming Girlhood

Henry Wadsworth Longfellow ~

"Youth comes but once in a lifetime."

FLASHBACK TO THE PAST

let's talk **A few years ago my mother and I went through a box of keepsakes she had gathered throughout my younger years. We stumbled on an hilarious, laugh-out-loud letter I had written her in fifth grade. The general theme behind the two pages of clumsy cursive boiled down to: "Mom, can I please, please get a bra?" My desperate plea was followed with a list of names of every girl in fifth grade who already had one. It concluded with the classic, "I am the only one who doesn't have one!" Sound familiar?**

The letter worked and I got my bra. It had to have been a triple-A cup size and probably stayed puckered for a good two years before I finally filled it out. I in no way needed a bra at the time, but that didn't matter. My friends had triggered the bra alarm; therefore, it was time to get one.

Another alarm would sound in sixth grade and I would begin that joyous and never-ending journey of shaving my already-to-begin-with- hairless legs. It was an unspoken litmus test of all things cool— in sixth grade, there were "shavers" and "nonshavers." Heaven help you if you were a "nonshaver," especially if your legs looked like the boys' legs.

And so it continued through the years. The alarm would sound and off we'd rush to get our first spiral perm, pair of designer jeans, brand velour shorts, bikini swimsuit, haircut with wings, *Seventeen* magazine subscription, boyfriend, or job. Every milestone signaled that we were leaving behind the "little girl" years and were well on our way to growing up. Just as is the case today with our own daughters, our timeline for "growing up" didn't always match our parents' preferred timeline.

PERSONAL reflection

What privilege, rite of passage, or item of importance do you remember approaching your parents about in your own season of girlhood? How old were you in each instance, and how did your parents respond to your request?

How did you feel about their response?

Overall, what was your parents' attitude when it came to other requests made over the years?

● Disengaged   ● Too strict   ● Well-balanced

When it came to experiencing privileges or standard rites of passage, where did you normally fall on the timeline relative to your peer group?

Among the first	Somewhere in the middle	Bringin' up the rear	Are you kidding? I'm still begging for a pair of designer jeans!

We can benefit from reflecting on our own girlhood years. Often we snap into "mom-mode" and forget how important some of these issues were to us when we were our daughters' age. Our daughters naturally want to experience the same milestones other girls their age do. Their greatest fear is to be the last in line or, even worse, not in line at all.

In hindsight, do you think you experienced something too early in your girlhood years? ● Yes ● No
If yes, explain and include your age at the time.

Do you feel as if your parents made a mistake in saying no or in making you wait too long for something? ● Yes ● No
If yes, what was it?

How might your answers to these questions influence your attitude toward your own daughter and deciding when she is ready to experience certain privileges or rites of passage?

GOD'S TAKE on the issue

Read Ecclesiastes 3:1-8.

Girlhood is a season of life and, just as the Ecclesiastes passage indicates, we are not given a specific time stamp on when certain milestones or activities should occur. We need to accept that it is perfectly normal for our daughters to look forward to certain "activities" or "experiences" often reserved for a later season of life. God wired them to want to grow up, and culture takes advantage of that desire by enticing them to hurry along the process. As parents, our role is to evaluate the request, pray for wisdom, and decide the best timing and course of action that suits our particular child.

One of the biggest challenges we will face in the parenting journey is when other well-meaning Christian parents differ in their parenting philosophies pertaining to the gray issues.

Consider some of the parenting challenges you face in which other Christian parents set different rules or boundaries regarding the same issue. List three that come to mind (Example: My daughter is 13 and her best friend is allowed to see some PG-13 movies, but my daughter is not).

1.

2.

3.

When you run up against conflict of opinion in parenting, how do you usually feel about other parents' philosophy?

(If your daughter is young and you have not yet experienced this challenge, answer based on how you think you would feel.)

- What are they thinking?!
- I don't understand their positions sometimes, but I accept that Christian parents can differ on various issues.
- Maybe I should rethink the way I do things.
- Never say never ...

Let me offer a word of caution: If considering other parents' approach on an issue has ever made you feel pressured to question your stance, don't automatically assume that you are not in the right.

Tomorrow we will continue our discussion on how best to balance our daughters' requests in the growing-up journey. Whether she comes a-knockin' with a request for boyfriend, cell phone, or thong underwear, at least you'll be prepared with some general principles.

If your daughter is still young (3 or younger), please do not feel that this topic is premature. Considering your parenting philosophy in advance gives you an advantage. Not to mention, you will receive great insight as you hear from other mothers in your group who have gone before you.

DAY 2

ON YOUR MARK, GET SET, GROW UP!

let's talk **In researching this topic, I conducted an informal survey, asking Christian mothers with daughters to weigh in on issues they've had to face as a result of the pressure on girls to grow up fast. Here is a sampling:**

My daughter is 11 and in 6th grade. I estimate that 90 percent of the girls in her class wear make-up.

My little one is hitting the pre-teen stage. She's 9 and wants to wear a bra.

I have a 10-year-old daughter, and she tells me every day she wants a cell phone and a Facebook page. She says everyone in her class has them!

When my daughter was 16, she asked to get her nose pierced and my answer was no. Now she is in college and would like a Christian fish tattooed on her foot. "No" again—we pay the bills!

Highlighting hair and getting fake nails is very common among 11- and 12–year-olds in our town.

My daughter is only 4, and my family and friends think my husband and I are too strict for not allowing her to watch shows like "Hannah Montana" and "High School Musical."

My daughter is 8, and I allow two-piece swimsuits—as long as they're not skimpy.

My daughter is 6. My husband was recently shuttling her and a friend in the car and said they were talking about cute boys. He was shocked when they used the words, "He is soooo hot!"

We just found out our 12-year-old daughter has a MySpace page. Her profile reveals she is 18, and includes her picture and a sexually explicit comment.

If you have a younger daughter, I'll wait while you take a deep breath. I realize it can leave you somewhat out of breath to get a foreshadowing of what may loom on the not-so-distant horizon. As we discussed in yesterday's homework, we must take care not to fall at either end of the extreme-parenting spectrum. Remember, our goal is to have some necessary conversations with our daughters, all the while drawing appropriate boundaries in an effort to better protect them.

Perhaps at times you have wondered why "a good Christian mother," trying to raise "a good Christian daughter," wouldn't just draw a firm line in the sand and issue a firm "No!" when approached with the latest issue *du jour*. Easier said than done. What I have discovered in parenting my own "good Christian daughter," as well as in ministering to many others across the nation, is this: Like it or not, many, if not most, of our "good Christian girls" are drowning in a sea of cultural pressures that cannot begin to compare to what we faced at their age.

PERSONAL reflection

Stop for a minute to think about some of the challenges girls today face that didn't exist in your youth. List some that come to mind.

What challenge did you face that might have seemed equally extreme to your parents?

What can you learn from your parents' decisions that you can apply to your own parenting skills?

A fine balance exists in drawing firm boundaries in some areas, while at the same time being willing to compromise in others. Girls who hear "no" over and over often rebel out of sheer exasperation with all the rules. I know this fact may be difficult to believe if your daughter is still young and doodling "I ♥ Jesus" on the front of her spiral notebook at school. Girls like that don't grow up and ask for thong underwear, right? Wrong!

CONVERSATION boosters

Read the following scenarios and find one that matches your daughter's age range. Write a script for the conversation you might have if your daughter was the one doing the asking. Feel free to try the other scenarios as well.

46

If your daughter is age 5 or under:

Your daughter has just watched her favorite movie, *The Little Mermaid*. She rushes off to her room to dig through her dress-up box and emerges minutes later dressed as Ariel. She wears a tulle skirt and a rolled-up T-shirt with her midriff exposed (like Ariel's) and proceeds to tell you that she wants to wear her outfit to preschool tomorrow.

You say:

If your daughter is 6-9:

You're shopping with your daughter and she's immediately drawn to the glittery summer offerings. She plucks a pair of knit shorts from the rack that display the word "Princess" across the buttocks. "Mom, all my friends have shorts like this," she exclaims. "These are the ones I want!"

You say:

If your daughter is 10-13:

Your daughter returns from a sleepover at the home of a church friend. When you ask her what they did, she excitedly tells you that her friend's big sister helped all the girls set up their own social networking pages after Mom and Dad went to bed. She says, "Mine is sooo cute! Do you want to see it?"

You say:

If your daughter is 14-16:

It's homecoming weekend and your daughter is going with a group of her friends, both guys and girls. She approaches you and tells you that everyone is going to the home of one of the girls for a pancake breakfast when the dance ends at midnight. Pick-up time is 1:30 a.m.

After calling some of her friends' mothers, you confirm that pretty much everyone is going. If you say no, you will have to pick up your daughter from the dance while her friends head to the party. Your daughter informs you that her life is "officially over" if you say no.

You say:

If your daughter is 17-18:

Your daughter is in her senior year and on the verge of heading out the door for college. One evening, when you duck into her room to kiss her good-night, you notice she is watching a popular show that has strong sexual themes and sends a strong hook-up message.

You say:

Believe it or not, I encountered all of the scenarios above with the exception of the social networking scenario with my own "good Christian daughter." Trust me, this is only a sampling of my laundry list of real-life situations!

BRINGING IT home

Here are a few tips I've learned over the years when responding to requests or situations that catch me off guard in parenting my daughter:

1. Don't act shocked.
Primal screams are allowed as long as they're done in silence. If you immediately react with a shocked expression and, "Why would you ask for such a thing!" your daughter may not approach you in the future.

2. Give her the benefit of the doubt.
Recognize that such requests/scenarios are part of the growing-up process, not a sign your little girl is growing wild. Consider responding with something like, "I could see why you would want to have/do this since your friends also get to have/do this." In making this statement you validate the normalcy of the request or action without endorsing it.

3. Resist the urge to hold your daughter to a predetermined timeline.
For example, if her older sister didn't shave her legs until she was 13, don't set it in your mind that 13 is the earliest age your younger daughter can shave. I had a friend in fifth grade who suffered greatly because her mom refused to let her shave her legs/armpits until eighth grade. She had hairy legs and was uncomfortable wearing shorts and swimsuits. The straw that broke the camel's back was when

some of the guys in gym class started calling her Chewbacca (the hairy ape-like character on *Star Wars*™). Her mother's defense: she was too young to handle a razor. Ironically, the scar to my friend's psyche was probably far deeper than any nicks she may have gotten from handling a razor.

4. When your answer is no, explain your concerns regarding the request.

If a Scripture verse/passage backs up the principle, be sure to share it, but avoid sounding preachy. Take the time to explain the "why" behind your rule. Don't exasperate a child further by only saying, "Because I'm the mother and I said so," or "What would God think of this?"

5. If possible, find a compromise.

This, of course, is only possible in gray-area issues. For example, if we apply this principle to the age-appropriate scenarios mentioned earlier, is it possible to let your daughter wear a green camisole under her rolled-up T-shirt? You could explain that real girls don't show their midriffs, but mermaids have different rules since they live in the ocean. Is it possible to say yes to a different pair of shorts or perhaps to allow her to wear the "Princess" shorts at bedtime in the privacy of your home? Is it possible in the homecoming-party scenario to say yes and offer to help the friend's mother with the breakfast?

Is it possible to kiss your daughter good-night without a word when she's in the middle of watching a show you don't approve of, silently asking the Holy Spirit to convict her heart? Remember, you should be having enough conversations with your daughter that, without a word, she is clear about where you stand.

6. When you do say no, try to find something else to which you can say yes.

Insisting that your 12-year-old not keep a social network page is a no-brainer, since it requires lying about her age to participate. The blow could be softened, however, if you extend another privilege to her in the meantime.

7. Get past the image-maintenance factor.

Resist coming down hard on your daughter and stifling her with legalistic rules rooted in fear of what other Christian moms might think. Opinions on what is acceptable and what is not do vary, particularly in gray-area issues. It's up to you to go back and forth with God and decide what's best for your daughter.

8. Avoid using a judgmental tone.

When speaking of other girls and mothers who have different rules from yours, do not trash them to your daughter. Which sounds more Christlike? "I don't understand why some Christian parents allow their children to lie to get a Facebook page." Or: "Man, with parents like hers, that poor kid is going to be messed up!" Father, forgive me for the times I've expressed that sort of harsh judgment.

Share an example (without mentioning names) of a parenting extreme in which the parents had too few rules/boundaries and the child's spiritual relationship seemed to be affected.

How would you have handled it differently with your daughter? Why?

Share an example (without mentioning names) of a parenting extreme in which rules/boundaries were too harsh and the child's spiritual relationship seemed to be affected.

How would you have handled it differently with your daughter? Why?

Read Psalm 25:4-5. How does this passage speak to your heart in the quest to find balance when addressing gray issues with your daughter?

End today's study by looking at your scripted answer to your assigned scenario. How might your answer change should you apply the response tips we discussed?

THE TECHNOLOGY INFLUENCE

let's talk **Ever wished, in this new age of technology, for a detailed chart with a timeline of when to allow each technology privilege and at what level? I know I have. To ban it altogether will almost ensure rebellion, and to allow it without limits will almost ensure danger. But if we are to parent with balance, we must come to terms with our love/hate relationship with technology and find a middle ground.**

One of my favorite sayings is, "It is what it is." We can wish technology away all we want, but it's here to stay. Truth be told, most of us couldn't live a week without it. What would I do without my cell phone to track down my kids or without e-mail to take care of business in a timely manner? I'm liable to break out in a rash if I have to look up a restaurant in the phone book and call for directions rather than Google™ it.

How important a role does technology play in your life?

Air, water, food, gadgets	I've gotta have 'it!	I can take it or leave it.	Technology? What's that?

How does your daughter's dependence on technology differ from yours?

One of the biggest challenges parents face is figuring out when (or if) it is acceptable to allow various forms of technology into their children's lives. For example, my oldest child didn't own a cell phone until halfway through ninth grade. My middle child received her first cell phone in eighth grade and her younger brother received his in seventh grade. The age of ownership keeps getting younger, and at this rate, I wouldn't be surprised if in another 10 years, babies aren't coming out of the womb texting on little pink and blue phones.

Many parents are completely caught off guard when their children begin asking to do/have this or that like the rest of their friends. Many of us just mastered e-mail and feel extra special if we know how to text message. As far as I'm concerned, you get bonus points if you can change the ring tone on your cell phone without relying on your kids to do it for you. Keeping up with the technology race is a challenge when our kids are moving from gadget to gadget faster than we can pay them off.

GOD'S TAKE on the issue

The Bible doesn't provide us with how-tos and don'ts regarding survival in this technological age. It does, however, give sound advice on what we should do when we feel at a loss for how to help our kids navigate the crush of electronic options that come their way.

Read 1 Kings 3:9. What did King Solomon ask God to give him?
- An understanding mind
- A harem of women and wealth beyond measure
- A palace with double-step crown molding and separate quarters for his mothers-in-law

Why do you think Solomon made this request?

week two RECLAIMING GIRLHOOD

As parents called to govern our children in their ever-changing technology worlds, we can find hope through this verse.

Summarize that hope.

What guides you in discerning between good and evil?

How can you model wisdom for your daughter?

We don't need to become experts in every form of technology in which our children engage. However, we need a basic understanding of the pros and cons in order to make wise and informed decisions about if/when our kids should participate.

Describe a situation in which you or another parent did not have a proper understanding of a type of technology that your/their child was allowed to engage in—with an unfortunate result for the child.

How would you have handled this situation differently with your daughter? Why might better foreknowledge of the technology have changed the situation?

Many of the unfortunate tech-related situations that have come to my attention boil down to a child who is pleading for a particular technology privilege until the privilege is granted. Often it catches Mom and Dad off guard and with little notice to evaluate the basics and teach their child to use it in a responsible manner. Further, Mom and/or Dad often fail to monitor their child's activity to ensure his or her safety.

List examples of unfortunate outcomes that could come from granting these privileges without proper training.

Giving your child a cell phone without guidelines for usage regarding minutes or texting limits:

Giving your child a cell phone with picture/video capabilities:

Allowing your child to use the family computer without parental supervision or monitoring software:

Allowing your child to participate in social networking sites:

Giving your child a gaming system or handheld gaming device with Internet access and failing to set the parental controls:

Giving your child an mp3-player and allowing her to purchase/ upload music without your guidance/permission:

Having no set rules regarding their use of technology via their friends' devices or at their friends' homes:

Taking a training-wheels type of approach is the best way to strike a healthy balance when it comes to technology. Just as you would never take your toddler off a tricycle and put her on a 10-speed bike with a simple push and a prayer, so is it not wise to allow your child to enter the fray of technology without training wheels. If you're not going to take the time to train your child, it matters little if she gets a cell phone at age 8 or 18.

Rather than focus so much on when our children are ready to experience certain levels of technology, perhaps we should focus on when we're ready to take the time to train them. Besides, the age of readiness for one child may not be the age of readiness for another. It's up to you as the parent to decide when your daughter is ready to enter the training-wheels phase for each tech privilege. There is no need to rush this process and the longer she remains disinterested in technology, the better.

Write James 1:5 here.

Most of our daughters will take their cues from their peers and when the alarm sounds for a cell phone, screen name for IMing, a digital camera, an mp3-player, or a social network page, they will have a tendency to follow the crowd. The truth is, many of us are swayed (or worn down?) when our precious little one sobs and tells us she is the "only one in her entire grade who is not allowed to have this-or-that or do such-and-such."

When was the last time your daughter tried a similar line? (If she's not yet old enough, get ready!)

What was the object of her desire?

Assuming that her age at the time of the request fell into the gray zone, what was your response? In other words, what sort of process did you use in making your decision?

(If your daughter is not yet old enough, choose an answer based on the response you would most likely have made.)

- OK, you caught me. She wore me down until I finally gave up and waved a white flag in surrender. I reasoned that if everyone else has a/gets to _____, then it must be OK.
- I told her that I would talk to her father about it, and we would pray and ask God to give us wisdom in deciding whether she was ready. My readiness/availability to take the time to train her also factored into the decision.
- I took one look at her and said, "Are you kidding me? Do I look like I was born yesterday? No __ -year-old is ready to _____. Come back in a few years."
- I called several friends who have daughters around the same age and asked their opinions. I based my decision on the majority opinion.

James 1:5 reminds us that God will grant us wisdom if we ask Him for it. Part of being wise is balancing a reasonable age of readiness with a commitment to engage in the technology for training purposes. When you determine she is ready, you don't have to allow her carte blanche privileges and load up the gadget with every bell and whistle or let her engage in the forum without supervision. Start slow and add privileges as they are earned.

For example, my kids started with a basic cell phone with no texting/camera/video privileges. They only had enough minutes to cover emergencies. Even after adding texting privileges, for a time I took my son's phone at night (on discovering that girls were calling at all hours). I also canceled the phone's ability to send/receive pictures and videos, even though a camera came standard and the feature was offered for free.

When it came to online chatting and engaging in the social networking sites, I set up my own accounts to get a better idea of the features offered and installed monitoring software on our home computer. I also required login and password information as part of our agreement, spot-checking my children's accounts on a consistent basis. I allowed my daughter to participate in social networking sites at 15 and my youngest son to participate at the minimum age of 14 because I remained fully engaged in the process. I knew that with my guidance and supervision, they would behave more responsibly at 15 and 14 than most college kids were behaving on the sites—many of whom, mind you, probably never received a moment's training from their parents.

As my children proved themselves worthy over time, I stepped back some from monitoring their activity and accessing their accounts to spot-check. When they were around 17, I ceased monitoring altogether. After all, they were nearing the time to leave the nest.

Remember, you are the parent and you set the rules. Your rules can be adjusted at any time and you can change your mind or reverse a decision. You hold parenting power and you know the ultimate Power Source. He is just a prayer away.

THE FRIENDSHIP FACTOR

let's talk **Benjamin Franklin once said, "He that lies down with the dogs, shall rise up with fleas." If you've ever had to treat a flea-infested dog, you know that it's far better to take preventive measures than to tackle the problem after the fact.**

"Bad company corrupts good character."

1 Corinthians 15:33

The type of friends your daughter chooses or gravitates toward can speak volumes about her developing identity. It's hard to say whether "identity determines peer group" or "peer group determines identity," but the point is moot. Either way, your daughter has willingly chosen to conform to a peer group and, depending on the nature of that peer group, it can have a positive or negative outcome on her behavior.

By the time your daughter reaches middle school, you will begin to see clues that indicate which girls in your daughter's peer group are on the fast track. If your daughter is a follower, this information could be predictive of what's to come. Nearly every peer group has at least one girl who is growing up too fast. As long as your daughter has other friends in her group to whom she can relate, who have similar rules and boundaries, she should be fine.

However, if the majority of girls in her peer group have their sights set on behaving like older girls, you may need to steer your daughter toward a new group of friends. If she is constantly exposed to the pressure to grow up fast and becomes the lone ranger in her group, you can expect some serious mother/daughter head-butting in the future.

PERSONAL reflection

Think back to your primary peer group during your middle-school and/or high-school years.

Do you recall a girl in your group who grew up on the fast track? If yes, what factors indicated her rush to grow up?

What, if anything, appealed to you about fast-tracking toward adulthood?

Did you give in to the pressure to grow up early or decide to give it more time?

How does that experience affect how you parent your daughter?

To this day I can vividly recall a situation I experienced in fifth grade. I hit it off with a new girl in my class, and when she invited me to spend the night one weekend, I pestered my mom until she agreed to let me go. I went home with Kristi after school on Friday and the minute I walked into her apartment, I sensed something wasn't right. Her mom left within minutes and told us to "be good and stay out of trouble."

When I asked Kristi when her mom was coming back, she told me her mom was spending the night with her boyfriend. Kristi pulled out a pack of cigarettes she had stashed in her bedroom and lit one. I remember taking one puff just to get her off my back, and I'm fairly certain the experience jaded me enough to never smoke another cigarette. I ended up spending the night because I didn't quite know how to get out of the situation without hurting Kristi's feelings.

Even without involving my parents, I knew at the young age of 10 that I would never return to Kristi's apartment. In fact, I steered clear of Kristi after that. I don't have to tell you that in a few years, this girl was big into drugs. My heart breaks for kids like Kristi who lack caring, responsible parents to protect and guide them through life. However, our schools are full of girls like her who are growing up on a fast track. As heartbreaking as their stories are, we need to keep these girls on our prayer list rather than on our daughter's friends list.

Which fast-track behaviors have you noticed among girls in your daughter's age range? Check all that apply.

- unmonitored computer access
- ownership of the latest trendy gadgets
- desire to wear/own expensive designer labels
- regular visits to a tanning salon
- hair highlights
- ability to see movies/DVDs rated beyond their age range
- permission to wear immodest clothes
- regular visits to get manicures/pedicures
- permission to wear make-up
- permission to purchase inappropriate music
- permission to participate in social networking sites prior to the minimum age
- frequent reading of fashion magazines
- frequent watching of TV shows geared to older audiences
- permission to wear thong underwear or padded/ push-up bras

- permission to hang out with older children/teens
- permission to go out/date boys at a young age
- permission to meet up and hang out with boys
- permission to participate in coed sleepovers or campouts
- sexual activity/promiscuity
- tattoos and piercings (other than ears)

Which poses the biggest problem for your daughter?

How did you handle (or are you handling) the situation?

GOD'S TAKE on the issue

Write 1 Corinthians 15:33 in this space.

Make no mistake about it, hanging out with people whose morals fall short of yours impacts your own values over time. This is not to say that your daughter can't interact with kids who don't know the Lord. In fact, it's imperative that she show Christ's love to them in part through relationship. Just make sure your daughter realizes that routinely hanging out with people who don't share her values can have negative consequences.

Give an example of a time when you or your daughter experienced the truth behind 1 Corinthians 15:33.

The National Longitudinal Study of Adolescent Health surveyed more than 90,000 adolescents on many health-related issues and evaluated peer influence (specifically related to teen pregnancy). The study found that, on average, a girl's risk of pregnancy decreased one percentage point for every one percent increase in low-risk friends versus high-risk friends in her peer group. The study also concluded that parents have a good reason to get to know their children's friends, as well as the parents of their children's friends. Researchers found that, with regard to a girl's risk of intercourse, her friends' closeness to their parents is equally as important as the girl's relationship with her own parents, because girls whose friends have poor relationships with their parents are at greatest risk for earlier sexual activity.[1]

Can you name your daughter's five closest friends?
● Yes   ● No   **If yes, list them.**

Can you name the parents of your daughter's five closest friends?
● Yes   ● No

Describe the relationship your daughter's friends have with their parents.

What can you do to know more about these relationships?

One distinction we make in our home is the difference between "weekday friends" and "weekend friends." A "weekday friend" might be someone my child meets at school or at an after-school activity. The friendship is primarily built during school hours or during the time spent in a common activity. Any time spent after school or on weekends is at our home in a monitored environment.

A "weekend friend" might be someone who has similar beliefs and values and is being raised with similar rules and boundaries as our child. I would not hesitate to have this child over on the weekends or to allow my child to spend time with the friend away from our house. Obviously, the "weekend friend" list is shorter than the "weekday friend" list.

Having taught our children this distinction, we have set a baseline for helping them choose a positive peer group that is "parent-approved." For example, if my child expresses a desire to get together with a "weekday friend" from school and we are unfamiliar with the friend, we require the friend to come to our house until we get a better gauge on the situation. The friend may or may not transition into a "weekend friend."

In some situations, our children had friends they strictly saw at our home because we did not have an adequate comfort level in allowing our children to spend time at the friend's house.

When you think about your daughter's current peer group, which friends fit in these two categories (if your daughter is old enough to get together with friends outside your home)?

Weekday Friends	Weekend Friends

What value can be added to your daughter's development by viewing friends in the manner we have discussed?

Sometimes it may be necessary to completely ban your daughter from high-risk associations (for a season or permanently). All three of my children on separate occasions experienced a major setback in their high-school years when a breach of trust occurred. As part of the consequences, the burden of responsibility was placed upon our child to earn back the trust before privileges were reinstated. In both situations, we identified certain friends who, because of a proven track record of distrust and a lack of repentance (or a desire to change), were put on the "banned friend" list—permanently, unless they could prove otherwise. This may sound harsh, but given the power of peer influence, we have a responsibility to protect our children and sometimes this means drawing boundaries that protect them from themselves.

Today, all three of my children admit that our "friend bans" forced them to reevaluate their faith as well as their alliance with certain people in their peer group. Had we not stepped in with a tough-love approach, I can only imagine how far off course they might have wandered.

If the girl your daughter is becoming doesn't line up with the young lady God created her to be, take a closer look at her peer group in an effort to get to the root of the problem. Your daughter will fare better if she has a high percentage of low-risk friends in her peer group. Girls who run with a fast crowd, by default, will grow up fast.

BOY, OH BOYS!

let's talk If my elementary school had offered a "Boy Crazy Club," I would have been president. I can't recall the exact moment boys appeared on my radar screen, but I'm pretty certain I can trace it to the "I like you" note I passed to Bill Anderson in fourth-grade homeroom. Maybe boys didn't make it on your radar as early as fourth grade, but I'm betting you have memories of when it did. As hard as it is to imagine, your daughter will chalk up plenty of her own memories when it comes to cooties, crushes, and all-things-boys.

 PERSONAL reflection

When did you begin to notice boys? Describe when your "cootie inoculation" wore off.

When did your daughter begin to notice boys and what were the circumstances (assuming she is old enough)?

How might reflecting on your experiences with boys affect how you parent your daughter as she begins interacting with the opposite sex?

In spite of the fact that this boy craziness is a normal occurrence in the growing-up process, most mothers are completely and totally caught off guard when it occurs, unsure how to respond or react. Should girls be allowed to "go out" in elementary school? middle school? IM, text, or talk to boys on the phone? Go to the mall or the movies with boys? Sit next to the boy they like on the field trip? What about when they hit high school? Is it really realistic that they could hang out in groups for the full four years? What does "Christian dating" look like? Is there even such a thing? Is old-fashioned courtship realistic? Seriously, where is the guidebook that delineates all these details?

I certainly don't claim to be an authority on what is and is not acceptable, but I'm happy to describe the position I hold on boy/girl dynamics throughout the growing-up journey.

My position has been a work in progress and what worked for one child wouldn't necessarily work for another. Depending on the temperament and level of maturity of the child, it has been revised along the way. Proverbs 15:22 says, "Plans fail for lack of counsel, but with many advisers they succeed." Just view me as one of many advisers. You know your daughter best, and what has worked with my daughter (and sons) may not work for your daughter.

BRINGING IT home

Young love: Elementary-school romances

Oh, how I wish an older, wiser mother had taken me aside and told me to take a chill pill when I labored over the episodes of young love in my home. In hindsight, when I think of all the hand-wringing I experienced over trying to decide if my fifth-grade son should be allowed to buy a girl a stuffed animal for Valentine's Day or whether my daughter should be allowed to send the boy she likes a note from summer camp, I want to slap myself silly. Trust me when I say that you can over-analyze some topics and this is one of them. When all was said and done, all three of my children experienced the thrill of "young love" at some basic level and had a few stuffed animals and love notes to show for it in the end. And shock of shocks, the world continued to rotate.

Middle school: The "going-out" experiment

I was pretty low-key when it came to the experimental phase of "going out." My mantra during those years was, "You can call it 'going out,' but you're not going anywhere!"

Of course, my children were required to hang out in groups and no couple time was allowed ... ever. With my two older children, their experimental "going out" phase was fairly uneventful and, quite honestly, resulted in their clamming up and talking less with the other person once the relationship officially transitioned to the "going out" status. Another rule I had in place was that they not refer to the other person as their "girlfriend" or "boyfriend." That tends to elevate the relationship to the world's level of dating.

However, let me state that my younger son had a slightly different journey with his "going out" experiences, since IMing and texting had become more prevalent in middle school and many of the kids his age were flocking to social networking sites and lying about their age to gain access. Because kids feel more comfort-able typing and texting things they wouldn't normally say to someone's face, it removed the natural barrier of awkwardness that was common when learning to communicate with the opposite sex. I encourage you to have some boundaries in place for communication with the opposite sex, regardless of whether or not you allow your child to "go out." I also recommend that you consider limiting or banning text messaging and possibly even taking the phone at night during these impressionable years.

High school: The date or not-to-date debate

If there is ever a time when you need to be extra attentive to your daughter's level of interest in boys, it's during her high-school years. Quite honestly, this is the season of life when her dating attitudes take shape. If you have not begun to lay the groundwork for what you deem acceptable and unacceptable, she will get her cues from the culture at large.

Having witnessed so many female casualties in my ministry to girls, I walked into my daughter's high-school years loaded for battle and ready to fight for a better standard. Of course, I was up against the challenge of finding that tricky balance in which you draw firm boundaries, yet, at the same time, allow for a little breathing room so she doesn't grow exasperated and stage an all-out rebellion.

Let's stop for a minute and take a deep breath. How does your parenting position on younger boy/girl relationships differ from mine?

What aspects of your daughter's emotional, spiritual, and physical development have you not considered until this week?

What actions (if any) will you take to adapt your parenting position?

One of the reasons I want you to think through your position and become comfortable stating it is because you will encounter a wide range of opinions along the way. While we don't have to embrace the opinions of others on this hot topic, it's important that we remain respectful.

Do you find that you get easily frustrated when other Christian parents have different standards for dating?
● Yes ● No   If yes, why does that happen?

Does your stance strengthen your commitment to your standards?

I want to give you a head's-up: If your daughter shows signs of early development, you could face a bigger challenge when it comes to keeping the boys at bay. Pushing the pause button in the rush to grow up is difficult when your daughter is already wearing your same bra size … or bigger. Girls who develop at an earlier age are often noticed by the older boys and treated the age they look rather than the age they actually are. As a mother, you will have to work overtime to minimize this effect. And certainly don't encourage the attention. I'm amazed at the mothers I hear from who brag about the male attention their daughters receive for being more developed.

Describe a situation in which early development brought early attention from boys. What challenges came out of that situation?

If you were the parent, how would you have handled this scenario? Whether you described a personal encounter or the experiences of another family, how could/should the situation have been handled differently?

In the book *All You Need to Know About Raising Girls*, authors Melissa Trevathan and Sissy Goff address the balance of gradually introducing your daughter into the world of boys and yet also allowing her "enough freedom at home to be able to learn to make wise decisions regarding boys so that when she leaves home she can take that wisdom with her."[2] They note that "if a girl has no prior experience with boys, casual or otherwise, this danger can be compounded" when she leaves home. The authors also echo my belief that "it is helpful for her to have already had practice in this kind of decision making while she still lives under your roof," noting that "the best time for girls to make mistakes is while they are at home."

They offer further wisdom in saying, "As she grows up, you can gradually widen the boundaries—giving her room to make her own decisions within the care of your watchful eye."[3]

How do you personally feel about Melissa and Sissy's statement above?
- Overall, I agree.
- I disagree. Dating has no place among Christian youth.
- I'm not sure. My position is still developing.

GOD'S TAKE on the issue

Write Proverbs 4:23 in the space provided.

How might we help our daughters "guard their hearts," while at the same time, help train them when it comes to navigating boy/girl relationships?

Read 2 Corinthians 6:14. What does this verse suggest in regard to believers dating unbelievers?

If we are having necessary conversations along the way with our daughters that outline a parent-approved model of dating, hopefully they will carry with them that same model and mind-set when they leave home. Even for the girls who make it through the high-school years without dating, our words will not be wasted. We, at least, will have provided a framework for when the dating opportunity presents itself in God's timing.

BRINGING IT home

In the DVD segment of this conversation we talked about
Ephesians 6:4 and the call to bring our children up in the training and
the instruction of the Lord while being careful not to "exasperate"
them. As we come to a close this week, reflect on the importance of
being a protector rather than a provoker when determining when/if
your daughter is ready for ...

Technology

Fast-track behavior

That next growing-up milestone

A relationship with a boy

End the week by praying and asking God to help you find the balance between being a "protector" and being a "provoker" as you tackle one growing-up landmark at a time. Journal some of the thoughts He gives you here.

CONVERSATION 3

Sex Is Great and Worth the Wait

Some Presentation Tips (3 BC's)

1. Be _____.
Confidence is a problem when we have _____
in our past. Be confident in God's standard and truth.

2. Be _____.
Constantly adhere to God's principles: "Be holy as I am holy."

3. Be _____.
Plan a weekend get-away. Other ideas:

Also give information to your _____.

The best time for girls to make mistakes is while they are still
at home. _____ your daughter for coming to you.

By 5th grade, they're being exposed to sex at some level, so start
broaching the topics. _____ _____of teachable moments.

God can use anyone and any story.

> **CONVERSATION STARTERS with your group:**
> ● What fears do you have in talking to your daughter about sex?
> ● How open are you about this subject with your daughter?

> Weekly challenge:

*Interested in reviewing this or other 5 Conversations Bible study sessions?
You can download all digital sessions by going to www.lifeway.com/women.*

WEEK 3

Revising "the Talk"

Jean-
Jacques
Rousseau
~

"Patience is bitter, but its fruit is sweet."

BEYOND THE BIRDS AND THE BEES

let's talk **A dear friend speaks very matter-of-factly to her children about the human body. When her children were young, she taught them the correct anatomical terms for their private parts, while I, on the other hand, provided my children with coded nicknames.**

My little nickname system worked just fine until one summer day when a new family moved into our neighborhood. I had heard they also had a six-year-old boy—the same age as my oldest at the time—so we stopped by one evening to introduce ourselves. When the mother introduced her son to my son, Ryan, I immediately knew we had a problem. Unfortunately, the boy had the same name as, um, well, you know (I still can't say it!). Anyway, I shot my son a pleading look to remain silent, but by the look on his face, it was clear we would have plenty to talk about on the walk home. I'll never forget his comment as we walked away: "Mom, why would anyone name their kid Willy?"

Drats. I had to come clean with him. It didn't matter though because the movie *Free Willy* released the next year, so the gig was up.

As you can imagine, I felt the tension when it came time to have the standard birds-and-bees conversations.

Describe what prompted the birds-and-bees conversation with your daughter (or with another one of your children).

 **PERSONAL** reflection

When, if at all, do you recall your mother having a similar conversation with you?

If your parent did share "the talk," did she respond to questions you had at the time or initiate the conversation on her own timetable? Briefly summarize her approach.

How old were you?

Over the years did your mother continue the conversations regarding sex? If yes, how often?

How has her approach influenced how you share or plan to share with your child?

As I mentioned in last week's DVD segment, it's time for a new and improved sex talk between Christian moms and their girls. If our daughters are to stand against the cultural tide, we must make "the talk" an ongoing conversation that begins when they are young and continues until they leave the nest. We must consistently relay to them God's design for sex while clearing up the lies they will hear about it along the way. And I dare say, that alone can be a full-time job.

Consider media messages you (or your daughter) have been exposed to during this past week regarding sex.

> What was the general message and where did you hear/see it (magazines, television, billboards, etc.)?

> Were you able to discuss the situation with your daughter?

Like it or not, our daughters are exposed to a message that runs contrary to God's design for sex. By the time they hear the buzz word *sex* for the first time, whether it be from television, a classmate, or an older sibling, we need to be sure we have provided them with a basic foundation of truth. It doesn't have to be complicated; in fact, the simpler, the better.

I love the approach that sexual abstinence expert Pam Stenzel takes in her book, *Sex Has a Price Tag: Discussions About Sexuality, Spirituality, and Self-Respect.* Here it is in a nutshell:

1. Humans did not create sex; God did.
2. Since God created sex, He is the one who understands it the best.
3. Since God understands sex better than anyone, a person who wants to have great sex (and why would anyone want to have rotten sex?) needs to know what God says about sex.

Stenzel then poses the question, "What does God have to say about sex?" The answer: Sex was created for one and only one situation: marriage.[1]

GOD'S TAKE on the issue

Read Genesis 2:24 and Matthew 19:4-5. According to these verses, a man leaves his father and mother in order to "become one flesh" with ...

- his friend(s) with benefits
- his long-term girlfriend that he will most likely marry some day
- his wife

Why did God limit sex to the marriage between one man and one woman for life?

God created sex to be enjoyed by a husband and wife within the exclusive boundaries of marriage. Only in this relationship can sex fill its divine purpose to seal the lifelong bond between husband and wife as their love brings about children whom they will nurture together.

If Christians are to believe and embrace what God has to say about sex, we've got to disregard all other opinions and decisions regarding the topic. We need to teach our girls that God's Word always trumps popular opinion.

Following are some secular opinions regarding sex. Circle the three you feel are the most common messages your daughter receives (assuming she's old enough).

As long as you love the person, sex is OK.

Sex is a normal part of life. There is nothing wrong with seeking to satisfy our desires.

What you do in the privacy of your bedroom is no one else's business.

As long as you're not hurting anyone, it's fine.

You'll know when you're ready. Just remember to be safe.

We were created with physical urges, and humans are no different than animals.

Always take a test-drive before entering into a relationship/ marriage.

It can't be wrong if everyone else is doing it.

Someone who is gay cannot help it. He or she was born that way.

The sad truth is, each of these damaging opinions is regularly taught as fact within today's fallen culture. In one form or another, assuming she's old enough, your daughter will hear them all.

Do you know Christians who embrace and attempt to rationalize any of these lies?

If yes, which ones do you hear the most? Go back and place a star beside them. What is the danger of adopting or excusing these philosophies?

First John 2:15-17 tells us, "Do not love the world or anything in the world. If anyone loves the world, the love of the Father is not in him. For everything in the world—the cravings of sinful man, the lust of his eyes and the boasting of what he has and does—comes not from the Father but from the world. The world and its desires pass away, but the man who does the will of God lives forever."

Do you think that God gives us desires of the flesh?

     ● Yes   ● No   ● I'm not sure.

How can we teach our girls to balance their urges with God's will?

BRINGING IT home

If your daughter is 10 years or older (or has begun asking questions about sex), have you had "the talk" with her at least once? If not, would you consider doing so sometime this week? If you have had this conversation with her, have you had it several times? A general rule of thumb is this:

By middle school, your daughter should be able to repeat back to you (in her own words) God's design for sex.

Take into consideration your daughter's age and then write a brief script outlining God's design for sex. Commit it to memory so that you can share it with her as circumstances arise. Remember, informing your daughter about God's design for sex is one of your most important tasks as a godly mom.

Script:

REPAIRING THE DAMAGE

let's talk **Once we have laid the foundation of God's design for sex, we can begin to build on that foundation and address the lies as they occur. Yet sometimes we moms can feel our strength draining away as we stand against the cultural tide. Even well-trained, good girls—those taught right and wrong from the cradle—seem to slip and slide on important moral and ethical issues regarding everything from honesty to chastity. In light of this trend, it's easy to feel as if we're fighting a losing battle. Particularly discouraging to me are the surveys showing that even a majority of Christians will end up having sex outside of marriage.**

While writing this week's session, I found myself feeling much like the laborers Nehemiah described who were trying to patch the wall. I did a radio interview with a major secular radio show to discuss a particular hit TV series among teenage girls (actually nothing more than an infomercial for casual, hook-up sex). Due to a sexually salacious ad campaign, the show—already the most watched series among girls 12-17—received a good bit of media attention.

My goal in doing the interview was to argue that over-the-top "sex sells" ad campaigns are irresponsible in light of the fact that more than 25 percent of teen girls has an STD[2] and nearly 40 percent of teen girls will become pregnant at least once before the age of 20.[3]

My point was clear: Ultimately, it is a parent's responsibility to monitor what their children watch, but many children don't have the luxury of having caring, engaged parents. I pointed out in the interview that in addition to the irresponsible ad campaign, the show failed to present an accurate representation of the fallout from recreational sex.

For example, for the kids whose parents are not monitoring their TV intake, what if 25 percent of the sexually active teens in the show contracted an STD and were forced to deal with the consequences? Or what if nearly 40 percent of the girls become pregnant and wrestled with that burden as part of the story line? Where is the representation of the 80 percent of teen mothers on welfare and struggling to make ends meet? Or how about having the girls wrestle with shame over a past abortion or a tattered reputation?

I presented God's truth while addressing the culture's lies, but rather than seeing any merit to my argument, the host began railing against abstinence-only sex education programs. He further told me that sex (even hook-up sex) is perfectly normal and that responsible and caring parents would provide their children with birth-control options, accepting that their children are going to have sex. Unfortunately, many grown adults adopt this worldly (and ridiculous) mind-set and are determined to peddle folly to our children.

GOD'S TAKE on the issue

Though sometimes it may seem as if we fight a losing battle, we should remember that God stands on our side when it comes to training and equipping our kids to live for Jesus. The following passage provides an excellent blueprint for Christian parents to successfully build on the foundation of God's design for sex while, at the same time, addressing the culture's lies.

> Read Ephesians 5:1-17.
> Summarize the following verses to develop a five-step action plan for helping your daughter align her attitude toward sex with God's plans for her.

Ephesians 5:1:

Ephesians 5:3:

Ephesians 5:6-8:

Ephesians 5:11:

Ephesians 5:15-17:

Ephesians 5 offers excellent guidance. If we want to counter culture's lies about sex, we must teach our children to be imitators of God rather than followers of the world. Only then can they understand that sexual immorality is not proper for God's holy people. We've got to warn our daughters and sons about those who will attempt to deceive them with false claims and assurances. They must not associate with such people.

It's up to us to faithfully point out the fruitless deeds of darkness by exposing them to the light of God's Word. We must tell our kids to be careful about how they live, making the most of every opportunity while seeking to understand God's perfect will.

Christian moms are obligated to help their daughters make the vital connection of why God set aside sex for marriage. It's not enough to read them the verses and tell them, "Save sex for marriage because God says so." Before your daughter enters high school, she needs not only a head knowledge of the verses of Scripture that clearly state that sex is for marriage but also to be well-versed on the dangers of ignoring them.

When telling your daughter that God desires she save sex for marriage, what reasons do/will you share to support why it is the best choice? List those that come to mind.

CONVERSATION boosters

Following is a comprehensive list of weapons I have used with my daughter to build on the foundation of God's truth regarding sex outside of marriage. Feel free to add any or all of them to your "arsenal."

Sexually Transmitted Diseases (STDs):

- More than 1 in 4 teen girls has an STD.[4]
- Forty percent (or nearly half) of sexually active teen girls has an STD.[5]
- At least 50 percent of sexually active men and women acquire genital HPV infection at some point in their lives. By age 50, at least 80 percent of women will have acquired genital HPV infection.[6]
- Most HPV infections have no signs or symptoms; therefore, most infected persons are unaware they are infected, yet they can transmit the virus to a sex partner.[7]
- Chlamydia remains the most commonly reported infectious disease in the United States. One in 20 women between the ages of 14-19 (4.6 percent) were infected, the highest proportion of any age group.[8]
- In the majority of infected women, chlamydia produces no pain, fever, or discharge. Because it often goes undetected, many women will discover they have it years later—when they can't conceive.[9]

Teen pregnancy:

- More than 40 percent of young women in the United States become pregnant one or more times before they reach 20 years of age.[10]

- Between 22 and 30 percent of teen mothers under age 18 have a second baby within two years after the birth of their first baby.[11]
- Only 40 percent of teenagers who have children before age 18 go on to graduate from high school.[12]
- More than 75 percent of all unmarried teen mothers go on welfare within five years of the birth of their first child.[13]
- The Alan Guttmacher Institute has determined that by age 45, 1 out of every 2.5 women in the U. S. has had at least one abortion.[14]
- Abortion is not a quick fix. A Guttmacher study found that with the passing of time, negative emotions such as sadness and regret increased and decision satisfaction decreased. That is, more women reported sadness and regret two years following an abortion than one month after the event.[15]

Future health of marriage:

- Seventy-two percent of all married "traditionalists" (those who "strongly believe out-of-wedlock sex is wrong") reported a higher sexual satisfaction.[16]
- Couples who don't sleep together before marriage and who are faithful during marriage are more satisfied with their current sex life and also with their marriages compared to those who were involved sexually before marriage.[17]
- Several researchers with the Heritage Foundation analyzed data from the 1995 National Survey of Family Growth and found that for women age 30 or older, those who were monogamous (only one sexual partner in a lifetime) were by far most likely to be still in a stable relationship (80 percent). Sleeping with just one extra partner dropped that probability to 54 percent. Two extra partners brought it down to 44 percent.[18]

Emotional consequences:

- The National Longitudinal Survey of Adolescent Health found that 25.3 percent of sexually active girls aged 14-17 reported that they felt depressed "a lot of the time" or "most all of the time," as compared with 7.7 percent who were not sexually active.[19]

- Another study of 6,500 adolescents found that sexually active teenage girls were more than three times as likely to be depressed and nearly three times as likely to have had a suicide attempt than girls who were not sexually active.[20]
- In a survey by *Seventeen* magazine, 91 percent of teens agreed that "a girl can get a bad reputation if she has sex." In the same survey 92 percent of teens agreed that "it is generally considered a good thing for a girl to be a virgin."[21]
- Oxytocin, a hormone that is sent from the brain to the uterus and breasts to induce labor, as well as to let down milk after a baby is born, is also released during sexual activity. This hormone is believed to initiate feelings of bonding and trust, whether between mother and child or husband and wife.

Which of these facts or statistics most surprises or shocks you?

How often does mainstream media give attention to these facts?

| Often | Regularly | Every Now and Then | Seldom | Never |

Given the information I have discovered regarding the problems associated with sex outside of marriage, I better understand why God designed sex exclusively for marriage and I am better equipped to explain it to others. It amazes me that one can find warning labels on everything imaginable; yet, when it comes to warning young women about side effects linked to out-of-wedlock sex, mum is the word.

Of course, that's where we moms come in. If your daughter is in high school, consider setting aside some time each week or planning a weekend getaway to begin covering these facts. Some of the facts can be (and should be) introduced in the middle-school years, if not before. Of course, all of them are worthy of repeated mention.

In any case, don't let your daughter act out of ignorance. One day she'll thank you for it.

REALITY CHECK: CHURCH KIDS HAVE SEX TOO

let's talk **Eighty percent of "evangelical" or "born-again" teenagers think sex should be saved for marriage. Unfortunately, there appears a huge disconnect when it comes to walking the talk.**

According to a study titled *Forbidden Fruit: Sex & Religion in the Lives of American Teenagers*, evangelical teens are actually more likely to have lost their virginity than either mainline Protestants or Catholics. Furthermore, they lose their virginity at a slightly younger age—16.3, as compared to 16.7 for mainline Protestants and Catholics. In addition, they are much more likely to have had three or more sexual partners by age 17 (13.7 percent of evangelicals as compared to. 8.9 percent for mainline Protestants).[22] Yikes.

Why do you think teens who are brought up in church so often become sexually active outside of marriage?

Equally as disturbing, evangelical teens scored very low on a quiz related to pregnancy and health risks. The authors of the study speculate that parents

of "evangelical teens" may be talking to their kids about sex, but the conversation is more focused on the morals rather than the mechanics. The articles further state, "Evangelical teens don't accept themselves as people who will have sex until they've already had it."[23] The author of the study notes, "For evangelicals, sex is a 'symbolic boundary' marking a good Christian from a bad one, but in reality, the kids are always 'sneaking across enemy lines.' "[24] The study also found that abstinence pledgers are considerably less likely than nonpledgers to use birth control the first time they have sex.[25]

No doubt, Christian parents are certainly in a quandary. On the one hand, we want to be sure our children are clear on the "why" behind God's mandate to save sex for marriage; on the other, we fear that if we give them information beyond that, it may convey that we are giving them "permission" to mess up. Add to the mix that half of all mothers of sexually active teenagers mistakenly believe their children are still virgins, and we have a real problem on our hands.[26]

PERSONAL reflection

If you were sexually active in your teenage years, do you think your mother was among those who believed her daughter was still a virgin?

● Yes   ● No   ● I'm not sure.

Why do you think mothers have a tendency to be naïve when it comes to their own children?

What can you do to prevent such naiveté yourself?

The truth is our Christian kids have the same raging hormones as the rest of the general population. Sometimes I think we imagine that our Christian kids will be exempt from such hormonal urges if we can teach them enough Bible verses and read them enough books on the matter. As mothers, our task is to equip our daughters with truth regarding sex outside of marriage and help them connect the dots to better understand the "why" behind God's standard of purity. It is critical that we continue to repeat and emphasize these truths over the years so they are clear about God's standard.

> In your opinion, what is the balance to giving our children informa-
> tion related to protection from pregnancy and STDs without sounding
> as if we are granting them permission or assuming they will have sex?

- Balance, what balance? Christians should only discuss sex from an abstinence position.
- Ninety-two percent of females will have sex by the age of 22-24, so we'd be crazy not to address the topic and give them information regarding safe sex.
- I have no idea where I stand. I am sincerely undecided.

Let me add an even bigger twist to the scenario. What if you discover your daughter is having sex? The sobering truth is that if she wants to find a way to continue having sex with her boyfriend (or hooking up), she will find a way, even while living under your roof. At this point, if you suspect she is planning to continue in sin, you are caught in a precarious position. The question then becomes, Do you or do you not encourage her to practice birth control?

> What would you do if faced with the decision as to whether to allow
> your sexually active teenager birth control (or how would you counsel
> a Christian mother who is facing this scenario)?

GOD'S TAKE on the issue

Read 1 Corinthians 6:18-20 as a review of what we learned from the DVD segment.

Reread the position you just stated (if faced with the scenario that your daughter is having sex outside of marriage or the counsel you would give another mother facing this scenario).

How does your position line up with 1 Corinthians 6:18-20?

My take is in line with Scripture.	I'm a little off, but Paul lived in a different age.	It doesn't, but what's a mom to do?

If it doesn't line up, does this change your position? If so, how?

The truth is that Paul's advice to the first-century Christians is just as applicable today as it was then. We can't make allowances for sin—especially in an area so important to our girls' health and futures. Doing so is never in the best interest of our daughters.

The evidence presented regarding the fallout from sex outside of marriage is reason enough to remind those who have already had sex of the benefits of second-ary virginity. (Remember, statistics show that nearly two-thirds of girls regret their decision to have sex and wish they had waited.) In this situation, I would highly recommend that a mother faced with this situation meet with her daughter on a weekly basis to discuss much of what we have learned thus far. In addition, she should draw boundaries and supervise her daughter as well as be very picky about whom she dates in the future (if she's allowed to date).

On the other hand, if after discussing the matter with her daughter, a mom discovers that she is unrepentant and unwilling to change her behavior, it is most likely because (A) she doesn't want to risk losing her boyfriend or (B) she has wandered from the path of God and is callous to His truth regarding sex outside of marriage.

Regardless, this mother must open the lines of communication in an effort to begin conversations about the information we have discussed. I would advise her to begin by praying for the right time and setting to approach her daughter. I would remind her that God can do a mighty work in her daughter's heart. Prayer is a woman's most powerful tool; while a mother may not be able to sway her daughter's heart, God can.

If I faced this situation with my own daughter and it was clear that she was not broken over her sin and was unwilling to repent, I would continue to focus on God's standard and not deviate one iota. God's Word reminds us of the standard: "Be holy, because I am holy" (1 Pet. 1:16). I would certainly not sit her down and go over a list of birth-control options because to do so, in a sense, says, "Hey, God's Word says to 'be holy,' but since you insist on being 'less than holy,' might I suggest a Plan B to help you cut your losses?" I could not say or do something that in good conscience would further encourage her to sin.

I realize that many Christians disagree with my position, but what's important is that we each go before the Lord and seek His guidance in the matter. If I have been faithful to educate my daughter about the fallout associated with sex outside of marriage and teach her God's design for sex, then I have been responsible with the assigned task. I will not be an accomplice to a decision that falls outside of God's will.

THE ADOLESCENT BRAIN: ACT NOW, THINK LATER

let's talk **For adolescents, a lag exists between the body's capability and the mind's capacity to comprehend the consequences of sex.**[27] **When we tell our adolescent daughters, "If you have sex before you're married, you could get pregnant," their brains are not cognitively developed enough to walk down a worst-case-scenario path and consider the full weight of teen pregnancy. Their bodies are saying "do it" and their brains have not caught up to say, "If you do, you might get pregnant and find yourself awake in the middle of the night with a colicky infant while your friends are at the senior prom." Nor are they able to see past the moment of desired pleasure to weigh the consequences of STDs, abortion, depression, and tattered reputations.**

This finding was especially helpful to me as I realized that I, personally, had somehow imagined my daughter had the same picture in her mind as I did when I would caution her about the risks associated with out-of-wedlock sex. We have to help our girls walk the scenario down its path and paint a picture of the consequences for them rather than assume they have the cognitive ability to do so on their own.

The best place to start is by showing our daughters how hasty decisions make for negative consequences.

Read the following verses and write their prescriptions (Rx) for not making rash, hasty decisions. I've done the first one for you.

Psalm 119:9
    Rx: To keep your way pure, align your actions with God's Word.

Proverbs 14:15
    Rx:

2 Timothy 2:22
    Rx:

How can you help your daughter see the importance of thinking through the impact of her decisions?

Teaching our daughters tools for wise decision-making and basic principles of cause and effect can help them better understand the importance of waiting to have sex until marriage; however, we can't rely too heavily on such tactics.

Valerie F. Reyna, professor of human development and psychology at the New York State College of Human Ecology at Cornell and an author of the study "Teenage Risks, and How to Avoid Them," cautions: "Younger adolescents don't learn from consequences as well as older adolescents do. So rather than relying on them to make reasoned choices or to learn from the school of hard knocks, a better approach is to supervise them. ... A young teenage girl should not be left alone in the house with her boyfriend, and responsible adults should be omnipresent and alcohol absent when teenagers have parties."[28]

What other wise boundaries should be in place to help adolescents avoid making rash, hasty decisions regarding sexual temptation? List all that come to mind.

In addition to providing our daughters with a foundation of God's truth regarding His design for sex, we also need to equip them with a plan to "flee temptation" or say no to sexual pressures. One study found that 41 percent of girls aged 14-17 reported having "unwanted sex" because they feared their partner would get angry if denied sex.[29] Another study found that even when the sex is wanted, it is often regretted soon after. In fact, the National Campaign to Prevent Teen Pregnancy in 2004 found that two-thirds of all sexually experienced teens said that they wished they had waited longer before having sex.[30]

Stop for a minute and think about the biblical counsel we give our girls to "flee temptation." How often do we go a step further and give them practical ways to "flee" or give them the words to say when they find themselves in a precarious situation? In my ministry to teen girls I have encountered countless young women who say they went too far sexually because they didn't know what to say in the situation. Again, this may sound absurd to those of us adults who are better equipped to put our thoughts into words. But for adolescent teens with raging hormones and little ability to think on their feet, it's a real and present problem.

PERSONAL reflection

Did you ever find yourself in a situation in which you felt pressured to go too far sexually? If yes, were you equipped to voice your boundaries in the situation?

Read 1 Corinthians 10:13. God promises our daughters two things regarding temptation. What are they?

1.

2.

Recall a time when God provided you a "way of escape" (NASB) in a tempting situation. Did you take it?

What advice can you give your daughter for knowing how to recognize when God provides a rescue?

BRINGING IT home

When discussing this topic with my own daughter, I encouraged her to come up with actual verbiage of what she might say when faced with a sexually tempting situation (a way of escape). As ridiculous as it may sound, I told her to practice her lines in front of her bathroom mirror, if need be, to be sure she has the speech down pat. Chances are, it's not a matter of *if* she will find herself in a tempting situation but *when*.

It can also be helpful to share a personal account with our daughters about mistakes we made in our past. I mention some specific guidelines to consider when it comes to when and how much to share, on *www.lifeway.com/5conversatons* and on my blog, *www.5conversations.blogspot.com*.

As a reminder, the focus should be an expression of sincere regret rather than a purging of the past for the sake of garnering emotional support from our daughters. We should not share anything until we are walking in victory and have claimed God's forgiveness.

If you experienced sexual sin in your past, are you walking in victory or are you still beating up yourself?
- I'm walking in victory.
- I'm learning to trust my past to God.
- I'm just can't move past it.

GOD'S TAKE on the issue

Read Romans 8:1.

Write the dictionary's definition of the word *condemnation*.

Romans 8 assures us that when we give our lives to Christ, we no longer stand condemned for our mistakes. Jesus forgives us and sets us free. In His eyes, those who have asked forgiveness are justified. That means that He chooses to accept us just as if we had never sinned in the first place.

If you struggle with feeling condemnation over your past, please stop right now and go before God. Ask Him to heal your heart. Consider telling an older, godly woman or mentor who can join you in your prayer for healing.[31]

If you are walking in victory over past sexual sin, write a sample script of what you might one day say to your daughter about your journey to healing and freedom.

I know I've given you quite a bit to think about today. End by praying that God will give your daughter a desire for purity. Pray also for the women in your study who might be coming to terms with their own past sexual sin; ask God to send an extra dose of grace their way.

THE BATTLE IS NOT LOST

let's talk **I am always amazed by the extreme focus many parents place on academics or extracurricular activities. Mom and Dad will take time off work to shuttle their daughters all over town (and out of town) for school or club sports, but when it comes to setting their alarms for church, forget it. Parents are exhausted by pouring their energy into things that won't matter for eternity and are left with little time to disciple their kids.**

It's no surprise that most of our Christian kids are behaving just like the rest of the world. Most of us are claiming Proverbs 22:6, "Train a child in the way he should go, and when he is old he will not turn from it," but the truth is, little training goes on.

As we end this important week, I want to leave you with a note of encouragement regarding teaching our daughters "the way [they] should go" regarding sex. Study after study confirms a direct link between engaged, caring parents and children who make wise choices. Don't ever doubt the power you have in influencing your daughter when it comes to sexual purity. One study indicated that teenagers in grades 8-11 who perceive that their mother disapproves of their engaging in sexual intercourse are more likely than their peers to delay sexual activity.[32]

PERSONAL reflection

Did either of your parents clearly convey their position on sex outside of marriage? If yes, what was their position and how did it impact your behavior?

Where would you prefer your daughter gain information about sex?
- At home
- At school
- On a date
- At church

In order of influence, with 1 being most influential and 4 being least influential, rank who you think is most influential in a teen's decision to have sex.
- Religious leaders
- Friends
- Sex educators/teachers
- Parents

The National Campaign to Prevent Teen Pregnancy conducted a survey that questioned 1,000 young people ages 12-19 and 1,008 adults ages 20 and older, and found that 45 percent of teens said their parents most influence their decisions about sex compared to 31 percent who said their friends are most influential. Religious leaders were only the most influential among 7 percent, while teachers and sex educators stood at 6 percent and the media at 4 percent.[33]

Many parents worry over the safe-sex message being peddled in many public schools. How might the above findings encourage parents whose kids are subjected to such a message?

GOD'S TAKE on the issue

Read Ephesians 4:17-19. How does the description of the Gentiles in this passage compare to the culture's attitudes about sex?

Read Ephesians 4:20-24. What does verse 21 assume about those raised in a Christian home?

Describe the specific course of action verses 22-24 detail regarding how believers should navigate life.

Paul's Letter to the Ephesians suggests that those taught about Christ hold a foundation of knowledge that helps them recognize the futility of the world's ways while giving them the tools to live in righteousness. Great news for moms devoted to teaching their kids God's Word!

BRINGING IT home

If we are to help our daughters learn to put off their old selves and put on the new selves, we need to regularly implement five essential parenting tactics. Let's take a look at them.

1. Keep the lines of communication open.

A key factor to raising daughters who desire sexual purity is to talk to them about it. A good rule of thumb to remember when it comes to discussing sex is to "keep the conversation simple and keep it going." It doesn't have to be complicated and, in fact, needs to be easy enough for a youngster to grasp. Many will begin asking questions about sex in grade school. (Remember Pam Stenzel's simple explanation from Day 1.)

It is also essential, when talking to your daughter, to provide a forum for two-way communication. One survey found that 88 percent of teens said it would be easier to postpone sexual activity if they were able to have more open, honest conversations about the topic of sex with their parents. Interestingly, the same study found that only 32 percent of adults surveyed believe parents are most influential in their teens' decisions about sex.[34]

Are you providing an opportunity for your child to have open communication with you regarding sex? How so, or why not?

2. Build the mother-daughter relationship.

One study found that teenagers who "report that their parents are warm, caring, and supportive—are far more likely to delay sexual activity than their peers."[35] Another unrelated study found that close relationships with mothers seemed to discourage youngsters from sexual activity. However, I should note that it also found that the effect diminished with age and, among girls, disappeared altogether. Author of the study, Barbara Huberman notes, "High levels of mother-teen connectedness were not significantly associated with delays in sexual intercourse among 10th-11th-grade girls." She offered the explanation that "girls in their late teens generally felt a powerful need to claim their independence, in part by defying their mothers."[36]

While this finding might be a tad discouraging to mothers with older teen girls, what does it imply to mothers of younger girls?

How should this affect your parenting style?

While I concur with Ms. Huberman's assessment that "girls in their late teens generally felt a powerful need to claim their independence," I'm not so sure I agree with her conclusion that many girls will do it for the sheer sake of "defying their mothers." It's important we not allow our daughters to push us away in these years and that we fight with everything in our being to keep open the lines of communication.

When my daughter was in her final years of high school, we made it a habit to go out to dinner together every few weeks. While broaching some topics related to sex was initially awkward, I found that her willingness to open up increased over time. Now that she has moved away to college, hopefully she will remember the topics we discussed, as well as the relationship we developed along the way.

3. Set boundaries and supervise.

Sarah Brown, director of the National Campaign to Prevent Teen Pregnancy, said that talk alone is insufficient. She further stated that what matters even more, especially among younger teenagers, is a relationship in which parents keep close tabs on them, knowing who their friends are and what they do together.[37] Amazing! Imagine that—deep down inside, our children feel more loved and cared for when they have boundaries and supervision! They want their parents to be their parents, not their buddies. Brown concludes that the ideal home for fostering this kind of closeness is one open to friends of the children. She said, "When a house is open to young people, there is this sense they can be themselves. There's food, space, caring adults around."[38]

> What are you doing to provide this type of environment for your daughter? (If she's not old enough, what will you do?)

When my oldest son entered high school, we added a game room onto the back of our house and declared, "This is the hangout. Your friends are welcome here." Six years later, with my youngest in high school, I could write a book on the benefits of that game room. Over the years we have come to love our children's friends as if they were our own. Many will come over and visit my husband and me, even when our kids are not home. Some of these kids are not believers and I pray for opportunities to share the love of Christ with them.

Significantly, we provided our children with a place to gather with their friends, all the while under the safe supervision of caring adults in the next room. You don't have to take out a loan and build a game room. I have heard of others converting garages into extra space or using their living rooms. All you need is one spare room and an open heart.

4. Feel confident in your daughter's ability to make godly choices.

A secular radio host once asked me in an interview, "Why is the Christian community so freaked out about their kids having sex outside of marriage?" It really got me wondering in the days that followed, "Are we freaked out?" The more I thought about it, the more I realized that our kids need to see us exhibit confidence rather than fear. If we do our part to confidently teach them about God's standards and are faithful to point out the lies of the culture along the way, we then can rest and leave the results up to God.

For example, rather than express fear to our daughters over contracting an STD or experiencing an unwanted pregnancy, why not simply state in confidence (as part of our ongoing conversations): "You know, honey, I have done my best to teach you why God designed sex for marriage and the fallout that can occur when you have sex outside of marriage. But the decision is ultimately yours. I can't force you to save yourself for marriage. God intended for sex to be enjoyed by grown-ups within the confines of marriage, so it's a decision that requires maturity.

"Having sex is a very serious decision and if you decide to have it outside of marriage, you need to be sure you are also prepared to deal with any fallout that may occur. In the meantime, I'm available if you need to talk and I'll be faithfully praying for you on the sidelines."

> How can you express confidence in your daughter's ability to wait to have sex until marriage? Or to adhere to second-time virginity?

5. Encourage her in the faith.

One major study that examined evangelical teens' outlook on sex found that 88 percent of those making virginity pledges end up breaking them. However, one group in particular stood out when it came to successfully keeping their pledge.

That group is comprised of the 16 percent of American teens who describe religion as "extremely important" in their lives. In other words, these teens are the radical believers who aren't afraid to walk their talk and are more concerned with pleasing God rather than pleasing others. The study found that when these teens pledge, they mean it. The study further found that the ideal conditions are a "group of pledgers who form a self-conscious minority that perceives itself as special, even embattled."[39]

> How might teens who view themselves as "a self-conscious minority that perceives itself as special, even embattled" behave differently than Christian teens who give in to the world's standards of purity?

> Read Galatians 5:16-21. What is the key to warding off the desires of the flesh (v. 16)?

> Read Galatians 5:22-25. What attitudes or actions in your daughter might indicate that she is walking in the Spirit?

Ask God to give you guidance on how best to arm your daughter for the battle that lies ahead. If your daughter is on the right track, ask Him to help her remain strong in her faith. If your daughter is on the young side, begin praying that she will see herself as set apart from the ways of the world. And remember, where God is present, the battle is not lost.

CONVERSATION 4

It's OK to Dream About Marriage and Motherhood

God's intent for marriage: _____ _____ _____.

1. Research indicates many young people get _____
   and _____ of marriage from their parents.

2. Many parents have almost _____ _____
   _____ _____ about marriage and often say nothing at all.

Many experience _____ _____ _____ in marriage.

Culture's negative attitudes _____ to motherhood.

Only 1 of 9 qualities related to _____ (having children).

All other keys to happiness related to _____.

Encourage your daughter: Look for a man who loves _____
more than he could ever love you.

   CONVERSATION STARTERS with your group:
   ● What is it about our culture that says you're better off
     on your own?
   ● How are you helping mount a new PR campaign for marriage?

   Weekly challenge:

Interested in reviewing this or other 5 Conversations Bible study sessions?
You can download all digital sessions by going to www.lifeway.com/women.

WEEK 4

Rekindling the Dream

Proverbs 31:28
~

"Her children arise and call her blessed."

THE DEVALUATION OF MARRIAGE

let's talk How I long for the innocent days when television depicted marriage in a positive light! One week of watching prime-time television reveals the media's attitude toward marriage: They either ignore it altogether or make a mockery of it. Rarely do we see a positive representation of the traditional institution of marriage.

A recent study of popular television shows found that nonmarital sex outpaced references to successful married sex by a ratio of nearly 3 to 1.[1] The Parents Television Council-sponsored study analyzed four weeks of scripted shows on the major networks at the start of the 2007-08 season, noting content including depictions of sex; implied sex; discussions on the subject; and visual references to strippers, pornography, and other aspects of sexuality.[2] They discovered that "references to adultery outnumbered references to marital sex by 2 to 1."

The "family hour"—the first hour of prime-time TV, which draws the most young viewers—contained the highest ratio of references to non-married sex.[3] "The notion that sex outside of marriage is inherently more exciting, more important, more worthy as the subject of story-telling, is a toxic message for parents and children alike."[4]

It's hard to believe it was once considered controversial for TV to show married couples sharing the same mattress!

"Her children arise and call her blessed; her husband also, and he praises her: 'Many women do noble things, but you surpass them all.' "

Proverbs 31:28-29

PERSONAL reflection

Name some TV shows you watched in your growing-up years that depicted marriage in a positive light.

Name some shows you watched in your growing-up years that depicted marriage negatively.

What evidence of the Parent Television Council's findings do you see in the shows that are on television now?

How might the shows you view contribute to your daughter's attitude toward marriage and family?

Television does reflect cultural trends; it's not always the other way around. But while I'm not suggesting that we send our TVs to the landfill, I do think we need to apply some general guidelines to the kind of content that enters our homes. We can't just say, "Marriage is great!" and leave it at that. We need to protect the way our children define and understand it.

GOD'S TAKE on the issue

Read Genesis 2:18. What does God say?

- "Solitude is the pathway to tranquility."
- "It is not good for man to be alone."
- "Man should embrace many helpmates."

In the space that follows, contrast Genesis 2:18 with this statement: "The surest way to be alone is to get married."

Read Genesis 2:19-22. Which "helper" did God deem suitable for Adam?

- An AKC registered, chocolate-brown Labrador Retriever
- A television loaded with every sports channel imaginable, his own remote control, and a lifetime supply of buffalo wings
- A woman whom He bore from a rib that He took from Adam's side

Fill in the blank for Genesis 2:23.
"The man said, 'This is now bone of my bones and flesh of my flesh; she shall be called "_____," for she was taken out of man.' "

Does God make allowances for any marriage relationship outside that of one man and one woman married to each other for life?

- Yes
- No
- I'm not sure.
- It doesn't matter.

According to a preliminary study by The Barna Group, less than half of 18- to 29-year-old born-again Christians favor a constitutional amendment banning gay marriage.[5] But make no mistake: God does not approve "marriages" between people of the same sex, regardless of what the government says about them. Our daughters are growing up in a generation in which the majority of their Christian peers line up with the world's way of thinking when it comes to the institution of marriage. The media relentlessly showers our children with the message that homosexuality is just as normal as heterosexuality.

In the course of writing this week's material, I turned on the television during a break to catch the noontime news. I could hardly believe it when the scene that greeted me was of two men making out on one of the soap operas. When I quickly switched the channel to my favorite national news program, the reporter was happily explaining that celebrities Ellen Degeneres and her longtime partner, Portia de Rossi, had tied the knot in Beverly Hills, California.[6]

As if that were not enough, the next morning I read this headline while drinking my coffee and catching up on top news stories online: "Hallmark Begins Selling Same-Sex Wedding Cards."[7]

PERSONAL reflection

Why do you think some self-proclaiming Christians believe that gay marriage should be a legal and recognized form of marriage?

God is the author and creator of marriage. He designed the lifelong marriage relationship between men and women, knowing that this plan best meets the emotional, physical, and sexual needs of a man and woman who are in love, while also providing a solid home foundation for their children.

When sin warps the concept of marriage, we need to remember that marriage as God designed it is perfect. Marriage doesn't need to change with the times. We don't need to revise it. God got it right the first time.

BRINGING IT home

If your daughter is old enough to be exposed to this topic, I must ask you: Do you know where she stands on the issue of gay marriage? If not, consider reviewing the Genesis passage with her. It will be impossible to understand and appreciate the value of marriage unless she first sees it through God's eyes. We must remember that God authored marriage; therefore, He sets the rules. We can make no compromises when it comes to what constitutes a marriage. You either accept it for what God created it to be or blindly follow the world's lead.

When discussing the issue with your daughter, be sensitive to the fact that the gay-friendly environment has encouraged many youth to "come out of the closet," and she likely knows someone who has done so. Approach the issue with a healthy balance of helping her hate the sin while showing compassionate love for the sinner.

Also, be aware that many Christian youth express confusion over the fact that gay marriage is often blamed as a primary cause for the assault on traditional marriage while the effects of divorce seemingly are minimized or ignored. Many wonder why the Christian community harps on gay marriage when so many of our own people experience divorce. It's a legitimate question and one we will address in the days to come.

End today's reading by praying that God will give your daughter "eyes to see and ears to hear" when it comes to understanding His intent for marriage. It's time to disseminate the world's dangerous message— one lie at a time.

MARRIAGE BUSTERS: HOOKING UP AND SHACKING UP

let's talk **A survey conducted by the National Marriage Project to gauge the attitudes of young singles regarding "mating and dating" revealed that sex on the third date (or a couple of weeks after meeting) is typical for a more serious relationship. "If you wait too long," says one guy, "they think you're not interested." In fact, one lingerie company is taking this warped "third-date" mentality to the bank in hopes of cashing in on the hook-up trend. Nicole Miller has created a line of sexy bras and panties under the name "3rd Date.®" Following is the description from their Web page of the lingerie line.**

"The '3rd date rule' is a cultural phenomenon found everywhere from nationally syndicated sitcoms to Internet blogs, and of course, your very own world of dating. ... The third date has become the societal norm when a woman will choose if she wants to take a casual relationship to a more intimate level.

"From its origins of glue stiffened linens and suffocating restraining corsets, to the 1960's rebellious 'burning of the bras,' to Madonna's 90's torpedo shaped power cones, lingerie serves as an effective barometer of female identity and is emblematic to the hoops which we have jumped through to attain independence and self fulfillment. The 3rd Date Collection® is not just about one night, one rule, or one moment. The 3rd Date Collection® is about women, relaxed and empowered in their personal and professional freedoms, choosing to dress in a fashion proclaiming their self-assertive sexuality. The 3rd Date® is a mindset, promoting a feeling of confident sensuality and well-being."[8]

Can someone pass me a barf bag, please? Where are the lingerie companies creating a sexy line of lingerie for the honeymoon? I remember when girls didn't set foot in a Victoria's Secret® store until they were wearing engagement rings.

In the description of the 3rd Date® line of lingerie, underline phrases that put a positive spin on "hooking-up." (Example: "societal norm")

What advice does the company offer women whose relationships never progress past the casual sex they encourage?

What advice does the company offer women who contract STDs or are faced with an unplanned pregnancy as a result of "proclaiming their self-assertive sexuality"?

As long as our culture continues to peddle the pro hook-up message and leads our girls to believe it an expression of "girl power," plenty of young women will oblige the boys with casual sex. If, however, the guys get the benefits of sex, honeymoon lingerie, and plenty of girls who happily shed their clothes and morals by the third date, what exactly do they have to look forward to in marriage?

PERSONAL reflection

As a girl, what aspects of marriage appealed to you?

Do you think your daughter's answers would align with yours?
Explain.

How can we ensure that our daughter's hopes and expectations
of marriage align with God's design?

Sexual desire between husbands and wives is right, and those feelings can naturally accompany a serious dating relationship too. The problem comes when we compromise God's plans for marriage and begin flirting with sex before the honeymoon. Girls need to understand that remaining pure not only honors their relationships with the Lord, but also serves to strengthen their appeal to a potential mate. Sadly, the element of mystery that used to accompany couples into their nervous first night together is disappearing.

Homemaking too has taken a tumble from its once-sacred place as a rite of passage reserved for newlyweds. A Rutgers University study on marriage found that most of the participants view cohabitation, or "shacking up," in a favorable light and almost all the men agreed with the view that you should not marry a woman until you have lived with her first.[9] Nearly 70 percent of those who get married first live together.[10]

What do you think most couples cite as the reason behind their decision to "shack up"?

- ● We hope to find out more about one another's habits, character, and fidelity.
- ● We want to test compatibility, possibly for future marriage.
- ● We want to live together as a way of avoiding the risks of divorce or being "trapped in an unhappy marriage."

The Rutgers study found all of the above among the most common reasons cited by unmarried singles.[11] Ironically, cohabitation actually increases the risk that the relationship will break up before marriage.

A National Marriage Project report states, "Many studies have found that those who live together before marriage have less satisfying marriages and a considerably higher chance of eventually breaking up. One reason is that people who cohabit may be more skittish of commitment and more likely to call it quits when problems arise. But in addition, the very act of living together may lead to attitudes that make happy marriages more difficult. The findings of one recent study, for example, suggest 'there may be less motivation for cohabitating partners to develop their conflict resolution and support skills.' "[12] Those who do go on to marry have higher separation and divorce rates.[13]

And whether they go on to marry their cohabitation partner or someone else, they are more likely to have extramarital affairs. How ironic that so many people opt to "live together as a way of avoiding the risks of divorce or being trapped in an unhappy marriage"; yet, in reality, the very act of living together increases their risk of an unhappy marriage!

GOD'S TAKE on the issue

Read 1 Corinthians 7:1-2. Why, according to verse 2, should "each man have his own wife and each woman her own husband"?

Why isn't cohabitation a valid option to satisfy the problem
of immorality and fornication?

Seventy percent of couples live together prior to marriage, so we can assume that
a good number of Christians are also making this choice. But what can we moms
do about it? What should we do to help our girls choose a better route? First, we've
got to pray, pray, pray for wisdom. After that, we had better do a lot of talking.

BRINGING IT home

If your daughter is old enough to understand, write a script of a
conversation you might have that could help her better understand
the influence the culture's "shack-up" mentality has on attitudes
regarding marriage. Emphasize how shacking up might discourage
young men from entering into a commitment of marriage. Encourage
her that the benefits of doing life and relationships God's way are
well worth it.

Script:

Brainstorm a list of practical things you can do to encourage your
daughter to avoid cohabitation prior to marriage.

UNHAPPILY EVER AFTER

let's talk **Nearly half of all U. S. marriages will end in divorce. Surprisingly, the divorce statistics remain about the same for Christians as they do for non-Christians. While most believers are somewhat familiar with that statistic, I find that few are actually talking about the consequences of divorce with their children. That's a problem.**

Approximately half of the women who will do this study have experienced divorce. My goal is not to "guilt" anyone over the decision but to candidly discuss divorce's impact on our girls' perception of marriage. Some of my friends have experienced the pain of divorce and I am the product of divorced parents (after 39 years of marriage).

If we truly want our children to experience God's best in marriage, we must educate them on the damaging effects of divorce. If you have experienced divorce, I encourage you to put aside the reasons behind your own breakup for the sake of informing your daughter about its consequences.

Which of the following do you think might summarize your daughter's view of marriage based on what she sees (or has seen) in your home?

- Given my parents' marriage, it's a wonder I don't join a convent.
- My parents shield me from the difficulties. Marriage looks like a piece of cake.
- I thought my parents had a healthy marriage, but I was completely blindsided by a divorce/separation that left me doubting the wisdom of a marriage commitment.
- My parents provide me with a picture of what God intended for marriage. They work through their differences with confession and forgiveness and model healthy conflict/resolution skills.
- My parents' marriage is anything but stable. I don't know from one day to the next if one or the other is leaving or staying.
- My parents hardly talk and never show affection. Getting married must mean kissing romance good-bye.

No matter how you think your daughter might answer that question, the truth is that even the healthiest marriage has room for improvement, and even marriages that don't last teach valuable lessons. In any case, it's important that we understand the impact our actions have on our girls, especially when those actions lead to a family split.

Judith Wallerstein, a well-known authority on divorce's impact on children, studied 131 people who, as children, experienced the divorce of their parents. In her landmark report, "The Unexpected Legacy of Divorce," she states: "Divorce is a life-transforming experience. After divorce, childhood is different. Adolescence is different. Adulthood with the decision to marry or not and have children or not is different. Whether the final outcome is good or bad, the whole trajectory of an individual's life is profoundly altered by the divorce experience."[14]

To what extent do you agree with Wallerstein's findings?

Totally agree	Somewhat agree	Somewhat disagree	Completely disagree

Explain your answer.

Whether you are the product of divorce, have experienced the conclusion of your own marriage, or witnessed the struggles of a friend, chances are you have seen the fallout divorce can cause. So why are divorces so common in America today? Well, popular opinion weighs heavily into divorce's dramatic rise in popularity. Even Christians buy into the notion that if marriage isn't lending to our overall happiness, it should be revised accordingly to fit the times. This comes from the incorrect assumption that God's ultimate goal is for humans to be happy.

Another factor lending to divorce's rampant social acceptance is the idea that it's impossible to know if marriage is for you unless you give it a try, and for some people, it may take several times to get it right.

The only way to make sure our kids don't buy these lies is to remind them that divorce is not the result of marriage being a mistake. God created marriage and He doesn't create mistakes. The problem of divorce isn't rooted in the institution of marriage, but rather in the people who enter into the institution of marriage. Divorce is the result of a fallen people making poor choices.

GOD'S TAKE on the issue

Though God allowed for divorce in the specific case of adultery, He never intended people to throw in the marriage towel over "irreconcilable differences" or as an excuse to walk away when flames of passion died down to a few sparks. Two passages shed important light on God's attitude toward the breakup of a marriage.

Read Matthew 19:7-8. Write Matthew 19:8b in this space.

Read Malachi 2:16. Fill in the blank with the word that summarizes God's outlook on divorce.
He _____(s) it.

Christians struggle over God's disapproval of divorce largely because we have bought into culture's lies that it's a couple's only solution for resolving big marital conflicts. Interestingly, researchers find that only 30 percent of divorces end "high-conflict" marriages,[15] a fact suggesting that many couples call it quits over relatively minor concerns.

The study further concluded, "Except in the minority of high-conflict marriages it is better for the children if their parents stay together."[16] Contrary to the popular wisdom that being "stuck" in an unhappy marriage is a sentence to permanent misery, the researchers conducting the study found that an astonishing 86 percent of unhappily married couples who "stick it out" have happier marriages five years later. Nearly 60 percent said that their marriage was now "very happy" or "quite happy."[17] Sounds like a good reason to hang in there to me.

Do you know of a situation in which a couple weathered the storm in an unhappy marriage and is now experiencing a happy marriage? If yes, describe the situation.

No doubt, many experience their fair share of hurt and pain in marriage. No one ever said marriage was easy. We must, however, put aside any hurt and pain we may have experienced to focus on God's intent for marriage. I know this can be a tricky balance. It may be necessary for some moms to be blatantly honest with their daughters and say, "You know, honey, I realize that Dad and I aren't modeling (didn't model) the best marriage to you, but the truth is, God intended marriage to be a wonderful thing." Such a discussion may mean putting aside pride and pointing out healthy marriages that perhaps could serve as tangible examples to our daughters. It might even be necessary to confess mistakes in an effort to dissuade your daughter from making the same ones.

Most failed marriages can be traced back to mistakes made by both parties and a failure to adhere to God's standards. When these standards are not followed, marriages can suffer and sometimes even fail. If this is your case, claim responsibility for the part you may have played and still speak highly about the institution of marriage. (If you are a Christian married to an unbeliever, remind your daughter of God's counsel for Christians not to be "unequally yoked," but do so in a manner that does not dishonor your husband.) Always remember that God can heal any marriage; prayer is an essential part of that process.

Read 1 Corinthians 7:11-12. What counsel did Paul give regarding marriage?

- Stay committed.
- Take a break.
- Run away.
- Get a divorce.

How do you think Paul would respond to our modern attitudes toward divorce?

If your daughter is at an age when she understands the meaning of the word *divorce*, what can you do to ensure that she knows how God feels about it?

BRINGING IT home

Whether or not your daughter has experienced the pain of divorce firsthand or through someone else, it is necessary to remind her that marriage is a blessing from God.

Write a sample script of what you might say to your daughter to help her reconcile the reality of divorce with God's intent for marriage. (If, after today's lesson, you are convicted that you may have played a part in leaving your daughter with a negative view of marriage, include a sincere confession in your script.)

Script:

I realize that some who are reading this may have followed God's standards for marriage and, for whatever reason, your once-godly husband chose to walk away or chase after a life of sin. I personally know several women who experienced this painful misfortune and my heart breaks for them. Even through such sour experiences, however, these friends have not allowed the pain to taint their attitudes toward marriage in general. They work hard to speak highly of marriage and to ensure that their children are not left with a negative impression. This balance is especially tricky when it comes to pointing out mistakes made by the other party. I caution you to refrain from sharing too many details or divulging information that could strain your child's relationship with her father.

For those of us who have experienced the blessing of a healthy marriage, do we ever speak highly of it in earshot of our daughters? How have you expressed to your daughter how much you value marriage? Does she see you exhibit affection and swap caring words with your spouse? Does she witness positive examples of conflict resolution, confession, and forgiveness between you and your husband?

No matter the state of your marriage, end today's reading by asking God to heal hearts scarred by divorce with His truth. Open the lines of communication about marriage with your daughter so that she'll grow accustomed to discussing it with you for years to come.

CONVERSATION boosters

Stay engaged in your daughter's life, and don't lighten up when it comes to drawing boundaries in dating. In addition, make a concentrated effort to speak highly of the institution of marriage and consider pointing out positive examples of godly Christian marriages in your church and community. Expose your daughter to healthy marriages so she can build a healthy perception of marriage while strengthening her anticipation of her own.

DAY 4

MOTHERHOOD: BLESSING OR BURDEN?

let's talk **My friend, whose triplets now attend elementary school, recently shared her frustration over strangers' comments regarding her children in their infancy. She was completely caught off guard by the negativity some strangers held toward multiples. The most common question was, "Are they all yours?" often followed with, "I'm sure glad they're yours and not mine!" Fellow parents of multiples share similar frustrations over society's attitude that babies are a burden and multiples must be even more so. In fact, one father of triplets got so fed up with the negative comments he would receive when out with his children that he began wearing a T-shirt that said, "Yes, they're all mine and yes, I'm glad they're mine and not yours."**

The attitude that children are a burden, interruption, or even an afterthought seems a common mind-set in our culture today. The devaluation of motherhood is peddled in media, movies, sitcoms, high school and college classrooms, and political arenas. Motherhood, once at the top of the average young lady's list of dreams, has been reduced to a mere afterthought by the culture—if it even makes the list at all.

Describe a situation in which motherhood was negatively mentioned in your presence.

Why do you think culture trends to frown on traditional motherhood?

GOD'S TAKE on the issue

Read Psalm 127:3-5. Which of the following does this passage use to describe children?

- a punishment
- a blessing
- a curse
- a heritage/gift
- a pain
- a reward
- a hassle
- an expense
- an interruption

Read Genesis 33:5. How did Jacob reply to Esau's question, "Who are these with you?"

Jacob introduced his children as gifts graciously given to him by God. The Hebrew word for "graciously" is *towb*, which means "to do or make good in the widest sense." Jacob realized that God had greatly and abundantly blessed him by sending sons and daughters to his family.

While I doubt that anyone doing this study would argue that children are a precious gift and motherhood is a high calling, it is important we not assume our daughters share the sentiment. While I am not suggesting that marriage and motherhood are God's will for every woman, I do believe we need to equip our daughters to measure culture's anti-family mind-set against God's Word. We need to give our girls permission to dream again about the blessing of marriage and motherhood.

PERSONAL reflection

How high did marriage and motherhood rate on your list of things you wanted to do when you grew up?

They topped the scale.   They fell somewhere in the middle.   They were at the bottom of my list.

How important do you think these milestones are for your daughter (assuming she is old enough)?

Very important   Somewhat important   Not important at all

How might your daughter's perception of marriage and motherhood:

Affect her future?

Affect your future?

What practical steps can you take to help your daughter learn to view a traditional family model positively?

Before you start to fear a future void of grandchildren should your daughter hold a low opinion of motherhood, know that in spite of the culture's negative attitudes regarding these topics, most women expect and hope that they will someday marry and have kids. The bigger problem is that many women believe that successful pregnancy is something they can put off indefinitely. The delayed marriage trend and/or the culture's emphasis on building a career first and putting off motherhood into their 30s and 40s leads many girls down a path that ends in tears.

A 2001 survey showed 89 percent of young, high-achieving women believed they would be able to get pregnant into their forties.[18] Another study found that women have an excellent understanding of birth control, but they "overestimated—the age at which fertility begins declining."[19]

Fast Facts

Following are some facts related to delayed marriage and motherhood.

- A healthy 30-year-old woman has about a 20 percent chance per month to get pregnant. By age 40, that chance is only about 5 percent per month.[20]
- At age 39 the chance of a live birth after an IVF attempt is 8 percent. By age 44, it falls to 3 percent.[21]
- The actual rate for successful birth using frozen eggs is closer to 2.5 percent.[22]
- If a woman conceives at age 38, the possibility of miscarriage has tripled, the rate of stillbirth has doubled, and the risk of genetic abnormality is six times as great.[23] Additionally, the pregnancy is more likely to be complicated by high blood pressure or diabetes, and the baby is more likely to be premature or have a low birth weight.[24]
- Women treated for infertility suffer from anxiety and depression as severely as patients who have been diagnosed with cancer or cardiac disease.[25]

The waiting rooms of fertility clinics burst at the seams with women in their 30s and 40s who believed they had nothing to worry about as they put off kids year after year. We don't see the heartache behind infertility visits, the tears shed over a failed procedure, the endless shots and pills required, or the money spent for a shot-in-the-dark "chance" at motherhood. But why are so many under the impression they can wait so long to start their families?

We continue to see celebrities who are pushing 40 and a baby carriage at the same time. These stars have money at their disposal to perpetuate the lie that babies come easily at almost any age. Dr. Zev Rosenwaks, director of The Center for Reproductive Medicine and Infertility, (world-renowned infertility clinic at New York Weill Cornell), said in a *New York Times* editorial addressing the problem of infertility:

> "The nonstop media parade of midlife women producing offspring is stunning. These stories are about the fortunate ones: they beat the odds—As an infertility specialist, I often see women—who have been lulled into a mistaken belief that there is a medical technology that will allow women to have their genetic children whenever they choose. In our eagerness to outwit time, the media have made a bestseller out of the freshly minted fiction of "rewinding the biological clock." We can't and we haven't.[26]

BRINGING IT home

The former director of RESOLVE, a support network for couples coping with infertility, reports: "I can't tell you how many people we've had on our help line, crying and saying they had no idea how much fertility drops as you age."[27] Moms, we have a responsibility to tell our daughters the truth to spare them from becoming one of the women crying on an infertility help line someday.

End today by thanking God for the blessing of motherhood. Sometime this week, find a way to express to your daughter the joy you find in being a mother.

In the space that follows, list the top 10 things you most love about being a mom and plan to share them with your daughter. If she is old enough to understand the issues we discussed related to delayed motherhood, consider sharing some of the facts mentioned earlier. Remember, you can positively impact your daughter's future.

NEWS FLASH: YOU REALLY CAN'T HAVE IT ALL!

let's talk **I was caught off guard by a comment recently submitted on my blog. "Anonymous" had a bone to pick with me over not working full-time outside the home. She read in my bio that I had graduated from the University of Texas in Austin, and she chose to pepper me with the following comments:**

> "A fine example you are to our youth! You don't even work outside the home!"

> "Why did you even bother to go to college? What a waste of your parents' money! They must be so disappointed."

> "And you claim to care about our young women! Did you ever work even a single day?"

Clearly, this woman was annoyed that she had to share the same air with women such as myself.

Perhaps you remember Gloria Steinem, one of the key leaders of the feminist movement that originated in the 1960s. Many argue she was a pioneer in shifting attitudes among women when it came to "women's liberation." While I commend the progress women made when it comes to equal pay for equal work, the message of Steinem and her cohorts went far beyond that. Much of this effort railed against the patriarchy and imparted that women's greatest joy comes from building a career and serving self—forgoing anything that threatens to get in the way.

Interestingly, Steinem herself eventually married in 2000 at the age of 66. In a recent interview she commented that female college students today are radically different than the feminist ideal she and others once envisioned. She states, "I've yet to be on a campus where most women weren't worrying about some aspect of combining marriage, children and a career."[28]

The culture has done a bang-up job of carrying the "You can have it all!" banner to our young women but has failed to actually tell them how to have it all and live to tell about it.

PERSONAL reflection

When you were in high school/college, to what extent did you consider the challenge of combining marriage, children, and a career?
- I worried about it constantly.
- I was sure I could function as Super Mom.
- I figured it would all pan out.
- I never considered it.

How did your parents influence your attitude regarding career and family?

Interestingly, many young women are taking note that the pursuit to "have it all" may, in fact, leave women with less when it comes to personal happiness and fulfillment. *The New York Times* reported a trend in which a growing number of college young women aim for full-time motherhood as a major career aspiration. Amazingly, the report focused on young women at some of the most elite universities in the country.[29]

Albert Mohler, a respected columnist, commentator, and theologian, commented on this trend in a blog post related to *The New York Times* article. He notes, "Much attention has been focused on career women who leave the workforce to rear children. What seems to be changing is that while many women in college two or three decades ago expected to have full-time careers, their daughters, while still in college, say they have already decided to suspend or end their careers when they have children. In effect, these young women are launching a counter-revolution to the trends of the last four decades."[30]

What factors may have caused this "counter-revolution"?

As we continue, please understand that my goal is to encourage mothers to honestly explain to their daughters that you can't really have it all. Juggling a career and family is hard work. I didn't say it was impossible, but we need to be honest here—it's difficult.

A survey by The Pew Research Center indicates that "in the span of the past decade, full-time work outside the home has lost some of its appeal to mothers." Among working mothers with minor children (ages 17 and under), just 1 in 5 (21 percent) say full-time work is the ideal situation for them, down from the 32 percent who said this in 1997. Fully 6 in 10 (up from 48 percent in 1997) of today's working mothers say part-time work would be their ideal, and another 1 in 5 (19 percent) say she would prefer not working at all outside the home.

Interestingly, today a majority of working mothers (52 percent) say that a mother working part-time is ideal for children. Three in 10 say a mother who doesn't work outside the home would be ideal for the children and about 1 in 10 (11 percent) say that a full-time working mother is ideal for kids.

The Pew survey also asked parents to rate how good a job they were doing as parents, on a scale from 0 (low) to a high of 10. Regardless of their employment status, most mothers tend to give themselves relatively high marks on this scale. However, the women who are hardest on themselves are full-time working moms. Just 10 percent of mothers working full-time give themselves the highest rating

(10) as a parent; another 18 percent place themselves at the next highest mark (9). At-home moms give themselves more kudos as parents; nearly 3 in 10 (28 percent) give themselves the highest mark (10) and another 15 percent put themselves at 9 on this 10-point scale.[31]

The study's findings show that the culture's definition of "having it all" has clearly left many women disillusioned. We have a responsibility to tell our daughters the truth, and, if the results of the survey are to be believed, 79 percent of women with minor-aged children, who work full-time, would prefer to work part-time (60 percent) or not at all (19 percent). Our daughters need to know that.[32]

GOD'S TAKE on the issue

Proverbs 31 paints a picture of how godly women should live. What most stands out about this woman to many modern western readers is her obvious industry. Not only does she help the less fortunate but she also keeps her hands in business.

Summarize the job descriptions presented in each verse.

Proverbs 31:24

Proverbs 31:16

Lest you think of Proverbs' "virtuous woman" as a career-focused girl, know that much of the chapter is dedicated to her tasks within the home. Verse 15 says, "She rises while it is still night and gives food to her household." Verses 19-22 explain that she makes clothes for both her family and servants, making each garment out of the best she has to offer. "She does not eat the bread of idleness," verse 27 adds, but "she looketh well to the needs of her household" (KJV).

The Hebrew word for "looketh well" in the King James Version of verse 27, is *tsaphah*, meaning "to peer into the distance." This revelation is essential to understanding God's desire for women. While God gives us abilities, talents, and wonderful careers, He expects us to use these gifts while keeping our eyes focused on the future.

Don't think I'm trying to steer girls away from using their talents in the business world; I'm not. My goal is to teach young women that all decisions should be made with the end goal of doing what is best not just for us but for our families—those beautiful blessings God entrusts (or will entrust) to our care. If our daughters are to someday become the kind of mothers who "look well to the ways of their households," we must "peer into the distance" on their behalf today.

BRINGING IT home

Which of the following steps can you take to help your daughter model her life after the virtuous woman mentioned in Proverbs? Place an X by all that apply.

- I can start trying to emulate the virtuous woman in my home and at work.
- I can encourage my daughter to pursue a career in a field that is also conducive to part-time employment should she wish to reduce her hours when she has children.
- I can discourage my daughter from factoring two incomes into major financial decisions (home mortgage and car payment), so that she is free to reduce her hours or stay at home full-time when she has children.
- I can encourage my daughter to develop a skill that can be done from home as a back-up to her education.
- Once my daughter has expressed a preference regarding a particular line of work, I can encourage her to ask women in that field about the number of hours required and their experience in trying to manage the job while caring for a family.
- I can teach my daughter to prayerfully consider the impact that each major decision will have on her future.

Each of these steps can help teach our girls that while careers are wonderful, they shouldn't be allowed to derail future family plans. As mothers, our role is to guide our daughters to think through their dreams for the future and help them examine whether they are realistic.

More importantly, we must emphasize the power of prayer and point them in the direction of the One who knows them better than we do or than they know themselves. Only by praying and asking for God's wisdom and direction will our daughters find balance.

Proverbs 16:9 says, "The mind of a man plans his way, but the Lord directs his steps." Whether or not marriage is part of God's will for your daughter, she needs to know that the most important relationship she will ever have is with Jesus Christ. When she makes that relationship her life focus, everything else will fall into place. Marriage and motherhood may or may not be a part of her life; but if her eyes are on Jesus and her heart beats first and foremost for Him, the outcome won't matter.

End this week by praying that you will have renewed excitement of God's view of marriage and motherhood and can adequately pass it along to your daughter. If moms don't give our daughters permission to dream, then who will?

CONVERSATION 5

Girls Gone Wild Are a Dime a Dozen - Dare to Be Virtuous

Bad behavior has been _____.

Will my actions today affect my _____
_____ tomorrow?

Reputation: the generally accepted _____
of somebody; character; standing; name.

We should be more about pleasing _____ than pleasing others.

If our daughters are to remember God's teaching and keep
His commands in their hearts, then they must be in God's Word.

You are making "_____ _____" into your daughter's
heart, a little at a time. God has a different _____ in mind.

CONVERSATION STARTERS with your group:

- How are you counteracting the message that
  "bad" is the new good?
- Where have all the good role models gone?

Weekly challenge:

Interested in reviewing this or other 5 Conversations Bible study sessions?
You can download all digital sessions by going to www.lifeway.com/women.

WEEK 5

Restoring Virtue

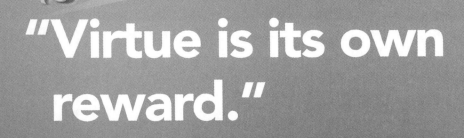

Marcus
T. Cicero

~

"Virtue is its own reward."

DOUBLE-MINDED DEVOTION

let's talk

While serving on an event panel for mothers of girls, I was asked: "My husband and I are throwing a sweet 16 party for our daughter in a few weeks, and we rented a clubhouse and will have a band so they can dance. My daughter is a good Christian girl who loves the Lord and is involved in her youth group. She came to us recently and warned us that we might not like the way she and her friends dance and said that they will be 'grinding.' I'm not really sure what it is, but one of my friends told me that grinding is simulated sex on the dance floor. Do you think this a battle worth fighting?"

This mother's friend was dead-on in her description of grinding and had the mother googled the term, she might have found the following definition on Wikipedia:

> "Grinding is a type of close partner dance where two or more dancers rub their bodies (especially the genitalia) against each other in a sexually suggestive manner. Grinding is a type of dry-humping, done to music, while both participants are standing. It is popular in the house and hip-hop dance styles. It is often performed at nightclubs and parties that play house and hip-hop music. It has also gained popularity at high school and middle school dances across the Western world, where there have been cases of administrators attempting to ban it."[1]

While most reasonable Christian mothers would put this matter on their list of battles worth fighting, the issue's existence reflects the duplicity we see today among "good, Christian girls." Such are the times when a Christian daughter can brazenly declare her love for the Lord in one breath and rationalize grinding in the next. Our youth are so desensitized to inappropriate behaviors glamorized by those in the spotlight that they believe bad has become the new good. It's up to us to reverse that unwholesome trend.

 PERSONAL reflection

In what ways have you seen bad behavior glamorized by the media?

Describe a behavior you engaged in and justified during your growing-up years—one that in hindsight you now know to be wrong.

Given the wisdom that comes with maturity, would you engage in that behavior again if given a second chance? Why or why not?

In Romans 16:19 Paul said, "I want you to be wise about what is good, and inno-cent about what is evil." Unfortunately, the notion of innocence is under attack. If our daughters are to be "innocent about what is evil," we've got to take action.

Place an X beside the steps you can take to help your daughter own the wisdom of Romans 16:19.

- I can stay engaged in her life and protect her from harmful influences.
- I must expose her to positive influences that will build on a biblical foundation.
- I must hold her school accountable for teaching her morals.
- I must regularly pray and ask God to put a hedge of protection around her.
- I must allow her to spend hours watching MTV in order to equip her to discern between good and evil.
- I must provide a welcome environment for her to share with me and communicate some of the pressures she faces.

If you hold doubts regarding the double lives many Christian girls are living, consider the social networking profile I recently saw for a Christian teen girl. Her status read: "In awe of the One who died for all." Unfortunately, the statement stood in stark contrast to pictures on her profile page where she stood among a row of girls with unbuttoned blouses and exposed cleavage.

While that example of double-minded devotion might be extreme, the truth is that each of us, to some degree, wavers back and forth in her commitment to the Lord. As mothers, it's up to us to make sure our daughters build their lives on a proper foundation of biblical truth. This won't ensure that they make godly choices 100 percent of the time, but it will give them a proper perspective of what behav-iors are considered good and bad in God's eyes. We must raise them to be critical thinkers, equipping them to use godly discernment when faced with choices that contradict their faith (like whether or not to participate in "grinding").

GOD'S TAKE on the issue

Read 2 Peter 1:3-9. According to this passage, what is the source of godliness and everything we need for life?

Is it possible to be godly apart from God?

● Yes   ● No   ● I'm not sure

According to verse 4, how do we escape the corruption in the world caused by evil desires?

Given what you've learned from the 2 Peter passage, what might explain the double-minded devotion we commonly see in today's Christian youth who behave in a manner that blatantly contradicts God's standards? Check all that apply.

- ● They are not utilizing God's divine power in their lives to escape the corruption of the world and their own evil desires.
- ● They lack knowledge of God and are not growing in faith.
- ● They may not be saved and therefore do not have access to God's divine power to live a godly life.
- ● All of the above.

Verses 5-7 list the qualities that we and our daughters should make every effort to add to our faith: goodness, knowledge, self-control, perseverance, godliness, brotherly kindness, and love.

Which of these qualities do you see manifested in your daughter's life?

Which of the qualities do you feel represents an area of weakness
for your daughter?

Peter encouraged believers that "if you possess these qualities in increasing measure,
they will keep you from being ineffective and unproductive in your knowledge of
our Lord Jesus Christ. But if anyone does not have them, he is nearsighted and
blind, and has forgotten that he has been cleansed from his past sins" (vv. 8-9).
We need to help our girls recognize the importance of growing in their relationships with the Lord.

Close today by praying that your daughter would pursue the qualities
listed in 2 Peter 5-7. Ask the Lord to show you things you can do and
say that will help your daughter in this pursuit.

AUTHOR OF VIRTUE AND ALL THINGS GOOD

let's talk

From the day we are born we experience a tug-of-war within our souls between good and evil. Through the sacrifice and resurrection of His Son, Jesus, God provided us with the means and remedy for rejecting evil and choosing good. However, we don't always utilize His divine power to escape the corruption in the world caused by our evil desires (2 Pet. 1:3). Paul, perhaps one of the greatest Christians of all time, recognized this frustrating truth.

Read Romans 7:15-23. To what extent can you relate to the struggle Paul described?

● Completely   ● Somewhat   ● Not at all

Our daughters, if they are Christians, also find themselves doing what they "hate" to do. Even those who wholeheartedly love Jesus sometimes fall into sin's temptation. But there is good news for all of us who face the battle. In Romans 7:24 Paul asked, "Who will rescue me from this body of death?" Verse 25 gives the Lord's answer to this question. It's a response that applies to each of us: Jesus Christ is our rescuer. Thanks be to God, there is a solution for our sin!

The challenge of writing and speaking about virtue and godliness is that I cannot make the mistake of assuming that 100 percent of my audience is comprised of believers. Until girls gain an understanding of sin and, more importantly, their need for a Savior, we can't expect them to behave based on "convictions" from God—those come only when a person accepts Christ into his or her heart.

In the early years we should focus on helping our kids connect the dots by labeling their misdeeds as "sin." As they get older, we can begin to explain God's solution for sin in a language they will understand. While we don't want to beat them over the heads and scream "Sinner!" when they misbehave, we have a responsibility to label their actions as God sees them. If at some point they don't come to the same conclusion as Paul did in verse 24, how will they come to the conclusion that they need a Savior to remedy their sin problem?

The goal of this final week is not to pressure moms to raise girls who are "good" but rather to help moms encourage and guide girls who are "God's." As we discussed yesterday, godliness is impossible apart from God. But when our daughters become Christians and begin the process of growing in their faith, we can find great peace in knowing that the Holy Spirit is alive and well in their hearts. He convicts them of the sin and wrongdoing in their lives.

If your daughter claimed Christ for her own after recognizing her own wretched state and desperate need of a Savior, realize that it is healthy for those claiming to be Christians to examine their lives and make sure there is some evidence of a changed life. In 2 Corinthians 13:5, Paul challenged those who were professing to be followers of Christ: "Examine yourselves to see whether you are in the faith; test yourselves. Do you not realize that Christ Jesus is in you—unless, of course, you fail the test?"

My children were young when they prayed to receive Christ, and God personally convicted my heart some years ago that I did them a disservice by "assuring" them of their salvation over the years. In fact, truth be told, it is downright unbiblical to allow them to assume that they are in the faith because mom says so. I have no way of knowing if their decision to follow Christ was a valid decision. Jesus Himself warned us that "Not everyone who says to me, 'Lord, Lord,' will enter the kingdom of heaven" (Matt. 7:21). We need to be careful that we don't hinder our daughters from taking a closer look at their lives to examine whether they are saved.

GOD'S TAKE on the issue

Read Matthew 7:17-20.

Complete the following statements according to the information given in the passage.

A good tree bears _____ fruit.

A bad tree bears _____ fruit.

What does Jesus' analogy of the good and bad trees suggest about those whose lives fail to produce good results?

Why is it important that we make our girls aware of this reality?

Before going on, understand I am not suggesting that a Christian is bound to do good deeds to prove his or her salvation; Scripture is clear that we are saved by grace through faith alone (Eph. 2:8-9). Good deeds will never gain us eternal life. "Good fruit" does not make one a Christian (a follower of Christ). It is, however, a sign that one might be a Christian. The absence of good fruit, however, may suggest that someone is not a believer. Followers of Christ will at some level be recognized by their fruit.

Paul Washer, preacher and founder of HeartCry Missionary Society, gave this illustration regarding the Matthew 7 passage. To the 2,000 students who had gathered to hear him he said:

"Let's imagine that I show up late and I run up here on the platform, and all the leaders are angry with me and say, 'Brother Paul, don't you appreciate the fact you're given an opportunity to speak here and you come late?'

'Brothers,' I'd say, 'you have to forgive me.'

'Well, why?' they'd want to know.

'Well,' I'd explain, 'I was driving out here on the highway and had a flat tire. I got out to change it and the lug nut fell off. I wasn't paying attention that I was on the highway and ran out and grabbed the lug nut. As soon as I picked it up in the middle of the road, a 30-ton logging truck going 120 miles an hour ran me over. That's why I'm late.'

'There would only be two logical conclusions,' Washer said to the captive audience, 'One, I'm a liar or, two, I'm a madman. You see, it's impossible to have an encounter with something as large as a logging truck and not be changed.'

'Many people today profess to have had an encounter with Jesus Christ,' he finished, 'and yet they are not permanently changed. God is way bigger than a logging truck.'"

Read Matthew 7:24-27. Those who hear the words Jesus spoke regarding good and bad fruit and put them into practice are likened to what?

- A wise man who built his house on the rock
- A foolish man who built his house on the sand

Those who hear the words Jesus spoke regarding good and bad fruit and do not put them into practice are likened to what?

- A wise man who built his house on the rock
- A foolish man who built his house on the sand

BRINGING IT home

Throughout this study we've discussed the need to help our daughters build their lives on a firm foundation of God's truth. The wise young lady who builds her house on the rock knows Jesus Christ as Lord. If your daughter is old enough to understand the concept of sin and the need for a Savior, consider going over the plan of salvation with her. (I have provided one on p. 164 for you to consider.)

Even if your daughter has professed belief in Jesus Christ, it's a good idea to go over the plan of salvation with her as a review. If you have any doubts regarding her salvation based on the fruit you witness in her life, pray for an opportunity to lovingly go over the Matthew 7 passage and other Scriptures we discussed today.

If your daughter is living a double life, it's difficult to know if it's due to the absence of Christ in her life (she is not saved) or a failure to respond to conviction from the Holy Spirit if she is saved. One possible assurance of Christ living within someone's heart is that when that person sins, he or she won't be able to carry on indefinitely in the rebellion. The same tug-of-war between the desires of the flesh and the Spirit that Paul described in Romans 7 gets under way.

If your wayward daughter is a Christian, you can be assured that the Holy Spirit is doing His part to convict her heart regarding her sinful choices. And following conviction, there should be (at some point) a godly sorrow that produces repentance, or a turning from her sinful ways (see 2 Cor. 7:10).

End today by praying for your daughter's salvation if she is not yet a Christian. If she professes to be a believer, pray for an opportunity to discuss with her the need to examine the fruit in her life in an effort to make certain her life is being built on a firm foundation.

PRINCESS TODAY, ROYAL PAIN TOMORROW?

let's talk **Chances are you find yourself caught up to some degree in the princess movement. Divas-in-the-making grow up wearing Onesies announcing their "Princess" status in rhine-stones. Disney made more than 3 billion dollars on princess paraphernalia alone in 2006 and, more likely than not, we all supported that fund to some degree.[2] While I don't think there is any harm in allowing our daughters to partake in the princess craze in small doses, we do need to be careful not to go over-board. If we do, we run the risk of creating self-indulgent monsters.**

David Abrams, a psychotherapist and licensed professional counselor, worries that the diva influence could lead to a sense of entitlement and that girls treated like divas, or temperamental superstars, could come to believe they deserve such catering through-out their lives.[3] I imagine that each of us, on reading that statement, can think of countless real-life examples of girls coddled to such an unhealthy degree that they morphed into royal terrors.

PERSONAL reflection

To what extent has your daughter been exposed to the princess mentality?

- Her exposure has been limited to fairy-tale books or movies and an occasional game of dress-up.
- I've got a diva living in my home and she's still sportin' some baby teeth! Help!
- My daughter put her plastic tiara aside years ago, but the attitude still remains.
- I'm a diva. My daughter's a diva. What's the problem?
- No divas reside under my roof.

When it comes to keeping up with the Joneses, modern girls find that the ante has been upped with 100-dollar-plus designer jeans, name-brand handbags, memberships to tanning salons, hair highlights, and pricey cell phones. Girls who base their worth on the approval of others feel pressure to conform to this ridiculous norm. Your little one may not be asking Santa for a Coach® handbag just yet, but if she's accustomed to making princess demands, watch out: It could be coming!

Indulging our daughters' inner princess requires balance. I'm not calling for an all-out princess fast, but the key is making sure our daughters don't let the tiaras go to their heads. If we are to ward off the dangerous side effects of self-indulgence and entitlement, we must make sure that we emphasize selflessness and servant-hood over selfishness and self.

If the indulgence of self becomes a year-round lifestyle, concern for others is on its way out the door. Take, for example, a recent study which found that college students are more narcissistic and self-centered than ever before. Five psychologists examined the responses of 16,475 college students nationwide who completed an evaluation called the Narcissistic Personality Inventory between 1982 and 2006. They asked for responses to such statements as "If I ruled the world, it would be a better place," "I think I am a special person" and "I can live my life any way I want to." By 2006 the researchers found that two-thirds of the students had above-average scores, 30 percent more than in 1982.[4] In other words, kids are growing up believing that everything really is all about them.

The study's lead author, Professor Jean Twenge of San Diego State University, said, "We need to stop endlessly repeating 'You're special' and having children repeat that back … kids are self-centered enough already."[5] The researchers attribute the upsurge in narcissism to the self-esteem movement that took root in the 1980s and further suggest that the effort to build self-confidence has gone too far.

Twenge, the author of *Generation Me: Why Today's Young Americans Are More Confident, Assertive, Entitled—and More Miserable Than Ever Before*, said narcissists tend to lack empathy, react aggressively to criticism, and favor self-promotion over helping others. Not surprisingly, when asked to identify possible remedies to the growing problem, the researchers stated that "Permissiveness seems to be a component," and that possible antidotes might include more "authoritative parenting" and "less indulgence."[6] It appears that narcissists are made rather than born.

> To what extent do you agree with the idea that warding off the problem of narcissism is more about "authoritative parenting" and less about indulgence?
> ● Strongly agree   ● Somewhat agree   ● Strongly disagree
> ● I'm not sure

> Basing your answer on what we've discussed throughout our study, how might parents practice more "authoritative parenting"?

> Why is it important that we do?

While in the process of writing the *5 Conversations* trade book and Bible study, I experienced some personal conviction over my own "inner princess" that at times has held me back from getting my hands dirty and feet moving when it comes to serving others. I took the opportunity to confess to my daughter that there may have been times where I modeled "too much princess" and "too little servant." We both committed to give the matter over to the Lord and are considering going on a mission trip together sometime during her college years. Also, in an effort to learn to say no to ourselves when it comes to our own wants and yes to others who have true needs, we decided to sponsor a child together through Compassion International.[7]

When we went to the site to see the pictures and short bios of the children available for sponsorship, we were moved by the number of children in need. I let my daughter choose which child to sponsor and she went with a three-year-old little boy from Thailand whose parents are farmers in an impoverished community. We split the monthly sponsorship fee, which amounted to $18 for each of us—the equivalent of one grande vanilla latte each week. We so look forward to receiving the updates and pictures about his progress and I often hear my daughter telling her friends about little "Aphichok" from Thailand and showing off his picture.

BRINGING IT home

One of the best things we can do to help build up our girls in their walk with Christ is to open their eyes to the hardships others face, instilling in them a sense of responsibility for those less fortunate.

Summarize James 2:15-16 in the space provided.

The Lord expects us to do for others. In fact, it's a privilege that grows us spiritually and can deepen our relationships with the Lord. Even if you feel that you adequately expose your daughter to opportunities to serve the less fortunate, consider activities you might participate in with your daughter to better expose her (and you!) to the blessing of giving.

Read through the following list and circle one activity you can put into practice with your child.

Volunteer to work in a soup kitchen or food pantry.

Sponsor a needy child/family at Christmas time.

Take a kid-friendly mission trip.

Participate in a canned food drive and have your daughter collect canned goods from neighbors and family members.

Collect winter coats for the homeless.

Have your daughter go through her toys, clothes, and shoes. Donate gently used items to a local children's home.

Ask your daughter to consider occasionally offering her childcare services for free to a single mother in your church (assuming of course, that she's old enough to baby-sit).

Encourage your daughter to donate some of her allowance to a missionary or missions cause.

Even if it is impossible now for you physically to go or financially to give, pray with your daughter for those who are less fortunate. There is nothing wrong with telling your daughter she's a princess and treating her like one on occasion. The key to doing so without harming her character is to consciously emphasize servant-hood above princess-hood. After all, tiaras aren't meant for full-time wear.

GIRLS-GONE-MEAN, CHRISTIAN-STYLE

 **let's talk** **Most of us experienced our fair share of girl politics (cliques, gossip, hurt feelings, mean girls, bullying) when we were growing up. We'd love nothing more than to spare our daughters the nonsense. As mothers, we need to be on guard and aware of situations in which our daughters may be targeted as victims, but we also need to be attentive to situations in which our daughters may be the perpetrators.**

Consider the following testimony from a woman in her mid-20's who was the victim of bullying during her growing-up years:

> "I wonder if people who really never experienced being on the 'other side' can really relate to this topic. I was on the other side of the cliques, bullying, and had some really horrible encounters throughout elementary and junior high. Today, when I share my testimony people look at me and say I never would have guessed that about you. Apparently, I look put together, but the insecurities from years ago still plague the way I feel about myself today. I constantly struggle with not feeling like I am good enough and it affects my relationships unless I make a conscious choice to rebuke the insecure thoughts.

"I was a year younger than my classmates, and I guess that made me an easy target. Kids took it to an extreme with me. I received threats, so much so that I didn't want to list my phone number or my address in the school directory because I was afraid they would hurt my family, me, or my pets. I wasn't the stereotypical kid that got made fun of, and I guess it goes to show that there isn't really a standard profile for a victim. It became such an issue that I had suicidal thoughts at the age of eight. At that point, your life is school and friends, and when that's falling apart you don't have the maturity and the coping skills to reason it through.

"I had an incident where a group of girls ganged up on me and basically attacked me. Eventually, I had had enough and I tried to kill myself, but thankfully I didn't succeed. I wasn't equipped with coping skills and at the time, I didn't have a relationship with the Lord. That was the furthest thing from my mind, since the 'Christian' kids were my main abusers.

"Today I am a Christian and find comfort in knowing I am fully acceptable in God's eyes, but I still struggle with the scars of abuse from my years of being bullied. I wonder if people are just being my friend out of charity or if I will be good enough for a husband. Most of all, I wonder if I will ever really grasp who I am in Christ. I don't have kids, so I can't speak as a mom. But I can speak by experience and I hope that maybe girls will grasp the impact their actions have on others at any age."

PERSONAL reflection

Describe a mean-girl experience from your past (whether you were the victim or perpetrator). How does that situation affect you today?

How big a problem do you think bullying presents your daughter (assuming she is old enough to encounter it)?

If your daughter tends to be a bully, why do you think she behaves in such a manner?

GOD'S TAKE on the issue

What grieves my heart the most about the testimony I received is that the woman states that much of her abuse was at the hands of "Christian kids." As important as it is to invest time and effort into protecting our daughters from mean girls (and we'll get to that), we must be equally as diligent in ensuring that they not become mean girls. We must have a zero-tolerance policy when it comes to our own daughters. One Scripture that addresses some of the components of girl politics is Galatians 5:14-26.

List trigger words from Galatians 5:14-26 that can lead to issues related to girl politics.

What behaviors and traits should characterize a Christian girl (vv. 22-23)?

In verses 25 and 26 Paul stated, "Since we live by the Spirit, let us keep in step with the Spirit. Let us not become conceited, provoking and envying each other." We moms can't force our daughters to choose good behavior, but we can encourage them to pursue behavior that honors the Lord, making sure that they perceive "provoking" and "envying" as sin.

BRINGING IT home

It is not uncommon for a girl to play the part of the "mean girl" at some point in her growing-up journey. Truth be told, we all have an "inner mean girl" who chomps at the bit for a little stage time. She can surface at any time—and at any age. Only by allowing God to run the show will we be able to keep her at bay.

Three steps can help rein in a daughter's inner mean girl, encouraging her to live by the fruits of the Spirit.

1. Ban cutting remarks.

No doubt we could greatly reduce the population of mean girls if more parents would take a stand and forbid their daughters to speak harsh words against others. Proverbs 12:18 reminds us that "reckless words pierce like a sword." When you tell your daughter rude and insulting words are not allowed, you disarm her by taking away her primary weapon of assault. She may attempt to pick up her "sword" when out of your sight, but a ban on harsh words at home can help reduce the chances that she will cultivate hateful speech as a full-blown habit. In other words, make it difficult for her to become a full-time mean girl.

2. Put a gag on gossip.

This topic is so obvious that it hardly requires justification. The Bible is chock full of verses that spell out the dangers of gossip. To the mean girl, "the words of a gossip are like choice morsels; they go down to a [person's] inmost parts" (Prov. 18:8). The more a girl ingests, the more she craves. Make it difficult for your daughter to gossip by having a zero-tolerance policy in your home. Hold her accountable when you overhear it and be very careful not to model it yourself. When you do stumble (we all do), own it and ask for forgiveness.

3. Know the difference between a peer group and a clique.

A clique is a toxic group of girls normally made up of one or two ringleaders and a multitude of followers. Of course, a clique wouldn't be complete without an unwilling victim. A peer group, on the other hand, does not constitute a clique. We should encourage our daughters to be nice to everyone, but it is unreasonable to expect that our daughters will develop a peer group that includes everyone. Just as we have natural preferences when it comes to developing friendships, our daughters too will prefer the company of some girls over others. In any case we should encourage our daughters to beware unhealthy "friendships."

Whether your daughter tends to be a perpetrator or a victim, consider setting aside some time to talk with her about the impact bullying can have and the resulting scars that can follow a person into adulthood. If you suspect she is the bully, talk to her about the value of kindness and make sure you model it toward her and others. Encourage her to step in when she witnesses someone being bullied and, if necessary, to involve a caring adult. It could be a matter of life and death if the victim is hanging by an emotional thread.

I realize that many mothers reading this have experienced the heartache and sheer helplessness over a daughter who has been the targeted victim of one or more mean girls. I wish there was a foolproof way to safeguard our daughters' hearts from such poisonous arrows. It is inevitable that our daughters will be the target at some level, so the wisest course is to equip them with a few basic survival skills.

First, bring the topic of mean girls out into the open. I know this is not a pleasant conversation to have, but it is only a matter of time before your daughter has a mean girl experience. If she is old enough, broach the topic with her and assure her that she can come to you if she is the target. You may have to assure her that you won't escalate the situation by overreacting; many girls avoid telling their parents for this very reason.

Second, let her know that most schools have safeguards in place to protect students from bullying. Encourage her to involve a trusted adult/teacher if bullying occurs while at school. It's always best if she can call it to someone's attention on the front end, rather than waiting until the situation escalates beyond repair.

This also goes for bullying that occurs at church. Unfortunately, the sad reality is that church girls dole out their fair share of venom—especially when they are not living by the Spirit. If necessary, involve the youth minister or the parents of the other girl.

In any event, encourage your daughter to be discerning about girls who fall into the mean girl category and keep a low profile or avoid them altogether. While I know it is not always possible to completely avoid a mean girl, do what you can to separate your daughter from bullies.

In Romans 12:18 Paul encouraged believers, "If it is possible … live at peace with everyone." I can't close this discussion without pointing out that sometimes "living at peace" with someone may mean breaking ties with them. I hear from many mothers whose daughters are bullied by mean girls in their direct peer group and yet they are hesitant to end the friendships. I've even had a few mothers share that sadly, the friend/bully is their daughter's only friend and she tolerates the abuse as the "lesser of two evils" (the other evil, being friendless).

Always do what you can to help your daughter foster new and better friendships with girls who appreciate her and treat her as a true friend, with respect. More importantly, pray that God will bring kind, uplifting friends her way.

End today by praying for your daughter. Ask God to convict her heart when she plays the part of a mean girl and to protect her heart when she is the target. Remind her that you are always there to talk it out. No issue is too small or insignificant to bring Mom's way.

WHOLEHEARTED DEVOTION

let's talk **I can't believe we're at the end of our study! As we reflect back on what we have covered in the past five weeks, the challenges can seem overwhelming. But the main truth—the bottom line I want you to take from this study—is that while we can't make our daughters walk in God's ways, we can help them build a foundation based on God's truth.**

I opened this week by talking about the problem of double-minded devotion among our Christian girls. While this concept may seem new, it reflects a struggle that has long marred humanity's inter-actions with God. In 1 Kings 18:21 Elijah the prophet challenged God's people who had adopted the worship of Baal—an idol approved by King Ahab and his wicked queen, Jezebel.

The New International Version translates Elijah's words this way: "How long will you waver between two opinions?" The King James Version says it a bit differently, but packs an important punch: "How long halt ye between two opinions?"

The Hebrew word used for "halt" is *pacçach*, meaning to hop, skip over; to hesitate; or to dance. The Israelites were supposed to live in devotion to God; sometimes they got it right. More often, however, they floundered in their faith and bowed to worthless idols and adopted pagan practices that only brought harm and heartache.

We live in an age in which Christians young and old, female or male, constantly hesitate over their relationships with God. Scripture offers us repeated examples of how half-hearted devotion to the Lord leads to unhappy consequences.

> To what extent does your daughter seem to "dance" between the ways of the world and the ways of God? Put an X beside the answer that seems to apply.
>
> - She follows the world with wholehearted devotion.
> - She follows God, but her devotion is split between the world's ways and His.
> - She follows God with wholehearted devotion.
> - It depends on the day of the week. She's sold out for God one day and back to following the world the next.

Our daughters are up against tremendous pressure to dance with the world. It bids for their attention day in and day out. As I mentioned, we can't make our daughters seek God with a wholehearted devotion, but we can certainly pray that they will. If our daughters are to stand a chance of countering the lies presented in the five conversations we have discussed, they will need to be undergirded by constant, loving reminders of God's rightful place in their lives.

GOD'S TAKE on the issue

To his son, Solomon, and the leaders of Israel who were to begin the task of building the sanctuary of the Lord, the aged King David said, "Devote your heart and soul to seeking the Lord your God." In 1 Chronicles 28:9-10 David encouraged Solomon to serve God with "whole-hearted devotion" and a "willing mind."

As Solomon and the people sought to follow David's advice and to honor the Lord, Solomon's kingdom flourished.

> Read 2 Chronicles 12:14 regarding King Rehoboam. According to this passage, Rehoboam did evil for what reason?

- He was jealous of Solomon's wisdom and riches.
- He didn't think it was important.
- He did not set his heart on seeking the Lord.

How might the contrast between Solomon and King Rehoboam compare to the challenge our daughters face today?

Are girls today doomed to repeat King Rehoboam's mistake? Why or why not?

Psalm 86:11-12 says, "Teach me your way, O Lord, and I will walk in your truth; give me an undivided heart, that I may fear your name. I will praise you, O Lord my God, with all my heart; I will glorify your name forever." If our daughters are to break down culture's lies regarding the conversations we have discussed, they must devote their hearts and souls to seeking the Lord with wholehearted devotion and willing minds. This is not an impossible goal. With the Holy Spirit's help, they can closely follow in God's footsteps.

Undivided hearts come when we make our lives all about God, acknowledging who He is and walking in what He says. In contrast, those who follow their own way and walk in their own truth will no doubt have divided hearts. They'll never give God wholehearted devotion until they see the need to change. While we can't make that connection for them, we can encourage them along the journey.

I can think of no better way to wrap up this study than to end it by praying Scripture over our daughters.

Look up the following verses and turn each into a personal prayer for your daughter. Then choose your favorite, and write it on an index

card to remind you that God's Word applies to every situation you
and your daughter can face.

Ephesians 1:17-19a

Psalm 24:4-5

Psalm 51:10

Psalm 141:4

Proverbs 4:23

Proverbs 28:14

Matthew 22:37

2 Timothy 2:22

Mom, your daughter needs you in her corner, praying that she will
remain grounded in the faith and wholehearted in her devotion to
God. The task ahead is great, but "Stand firm. Let nothing move you.
Always give [yourself] fully to the work of the Lord, because you
know that your labor in the Lord is not in vain" (1 Cor. 15:58).

A Plan of Salvation
to Share with Your Daughter

Your heart tends to run from God and rebel against Him.
The Bible calls this "sin." God's penalty for sin is death. Romans 3:23 says,
"For all have sinned and fall short of the glory of God."

Yet God loves you and wants to save you from sin, to offer you
a new life of hope. John 10:10 says, *"I have come that they may have life
and have it in abundance"* (HCSB).

To give you this gift of salvation, God made a way possible through His Son,
Jesus Christ. Romans 6:23 tells us, *"For the wages of sin is death,
but the gift of God is eternal life in Christ Jesus our Lord."*
Also see John 3:16 and Romans 5:8:
*"For God so loved the world that he gave his one and only Son,
that whoever believes in him shall not perish but have eternal life."*
*"But God demonstrates His own love for us in that while we were still sinners
Christ died for us!"* (HCSB).

You receive this gift by faith alone. Ephesians 2:8-9 says, *"For by grace you are
saved, through faith, and this not from yourselves; it is God's gift—
not from works, so that no one can boast."*

Faith is a decision of your heart demonstrated by the actions of your life.
Romans 10:9-10,13 tells us: *"If you confess with your mouth, 'Jesus is Lord,'
and believe in your heart that God raised Him from the dead, you will be saved.
With the heart one believes, resulting in righteousness, and with the mouth
one confesses, resulting in salvation. ...
"For everyone who calls on the name of the Lord will be saved."*

STONE UPON STONE

SESSION6

A Final Charge

Build a _____ _____ _____ around your daughter's heart while preparing her to stand on her own.

Nehemiah 4

Verses 1-6: *"What are those feeble Jews doing? Will they restore their wall?"*

Outside _____: Expect times of opposition from the enemy anytime God is at work.

Verse 6: *"So we rebuilt the wall till all of it reached half its height, for the people worked with all their heart."*

Our response is to _____.

Verse 10: *"… so much rubble that we cannot rebuild the wall."*

Rubble and remnant: Expect times of exhaustion and hopelessness.

The task _____ our abilities.

Verse 12: *"Wherever you turn, they will attack us."*

Expect times of opposition from within the walls, from fellow Christians.

Verse 14: *"Remember the Lord, who is great and awesome …"*

We have _____ _____ _____ _____! God tells us, "Remember Me!" _____ _____ _____ _____!

Verses 17-18: *"Each of the builders wore his sword at his side as he worked."*

Stone upon stone upon stone, you are building a wall of protection around your daughter's heart. The Bible, God's Word, is what we take into battle.

CONVERSATION STARTERS with your group:

● How has God helped you overcome times of opposition?

● What tools are you taking into battle?

Ongoing challenge: Keep the conversations going!

Interested in reviewing this or other 5 Conversations Bible study sessions? You can download all digital sessions by going to www.lifeway.com/women.

ENDNOTES

week one

1. Satkar Gidda. "Attracting Consumers Through Package and Product Innovation" [online] 23 May 2005 [cited 17 September 2008]. Available from the Internet: *http://www.brandchannel.com/brand_speak.asp?bs_id=111*.
2. Anastasia Goodstein. "What Can Industry Do to Stop The Onslaught?" The Huffington Post. [online] 2 October 2007 [cited 17 September 2008]. Available from the Internet: *http://www.huffingtonpost.com/anastasia-goodstein/what-can-industry-do-to-s_b_66798.html*
3. Ibid.
4. Joan Jacobs Brumberg. *The Body Project: An Intimate History of American Girls.* (New York, NY: Knopf Publishing Group, 1998), xxi.
5. Tracey Powell. "Body-scanning kiosk wows apparel shoppers." [online] 2008 [cited 17 September 2008]. Available from the Internet: *http://www.selfservice-world.com/article.php?id=16541*
6. April Holladay. "Women's Sizes by Country" USA Today. [online] 4 December 2004 [cited 17 September 2008]. Available from the Internet: *http://www.usatoday.com/tech/columnist/aprilholladay/2006-12-04-size-age_x.htm*.
7. Francis Crocker. "Time to realize the hourglass figure is past." [online] 21 November 2005 [cited 17 September 2008]. Available from the Internet: *http://www.ncsu.edu/news/dailyclips/1105/112205.htm#DJ4*.
8. Ginny Olson. *Teenage Girls: Exploring Issues Adolescent Girls Face and Strategies to Help Them* (Grand Rapids, MI: Zondervan, 2006). 55.
9. Sarah Baicker. "For teens, obesity no laughing matter." [online] 23 October 2007 [cited 22 September 2008]. Available from the Internet: *http://news.medill.northwestern.edu/washington/news.aspx?id=66261&print=1*
10. Ibid.
11. Ibid.
12. Hollie McKay. "Pop Tarts: Mariah Carey's Backstage Ordeal at Idol." [online] 18 April 2008 [cited 6 January 2009]. Available from the Internet: *http://www.foxnews.com/story/0,2933,351701,00.html*
13. Available from the Internet: *http://www.dove.org/*
14. Olson, 53.
15. APA Press Release [online] 19 February 2007 [cited 6 January 2009]. Available from the Internet: *http://www.apa.org/releases/sexualization.html*
16. Ibid.
17. Ibid.
18. Shaunti Feldman. *For Young Women Only* (New York: Multnomah Books, 2006).
19. Available from the Internet: *http://www.dove.org/*
20. Ibid.

week two

1. Anita M. Smith. "For Parents" The Institute for Youth Development; [online] 2004 [cited 25 September 2008]. Available from the Internet: *http://www.youth-development.org/articles/fp109901.htm*.
2. Melissa Trevathan and Sissy Goff. *All You Need to Know About Raising Girls.* (Grand Rapids, MI: Zondervan, 2007), 162.
3. Ibid.

week three

1. Pam Stenzel, Rick Bundschuh, Steven Case, Crystal Kirgiss. *Sex Has a Price Tag: Discussions About Sexuality, Spirituality, and Self-Respect.* (Grand Rapids, MI: Zondervan, 2003), 23.
2. "One in 4 teen girls has sexually transmitted disease" by The Associated Press [online] 11 March 2008 [cited 25 September 2008]. Available from the Internet: *http://www.msnbc.msn.com/id/23574940/*.
3. "A Summary of the Findings from the National Omnibus Survey Questions about Teen Pregnancyî by Princeton Survey Research Associates. [online] May 1997 [cited 25 September 2008]. Available from the Internet: *http://www.welfareacademy.org/conf/past/brown3.shtml*.
4. "One in 4 teen girls has sexually transmitted disease."
5. Ibid.
6. "HPV infection and cervical infection" from the American Cancer Society. [online] n.d. [cited 25 September 2008]. Available from the Internet: *http://www.drassad.com/Pt_Education/HPV%20infection%20and%20cervical%20cancer.pdf*.
7. Ibid.
8. "Chlamydia: Fact Sheet." Center for Disease Control and Prevention. Atlanta, GA. [online] 20 December 2007 [cited 26 September 2008]. Available from the Internet: http://www.cdc.gov/std/chlamydia/default.htm.
9. Miriam Grossman. *Unprotected: A Campus Psychiatrist Reveals How Political Correctness in Her Profession Endangers Every Student* (Santa Cruz, CA: Sentinel, 2007), 110.
10. Ibid.
11. "Teenage Pregnancy." March of Dimes Foundation [online] 2008 [cited 27 September 2008]. Available from the Internet: *http://www.marchofdimes.com/professionals/14332_1159.asp*.
12. Ibid.
13. Ibid.
14. "Abortion" The Guttmacher Institute [online] 2008 [cited 27 September 2008]. Available from the Internet: *http://www.guttmacher.org/sections/abortion.php*
15. Ibid.

16. David Larson and Mary Ann Mayo, "Believe Well, Live Well." Family Research Council [online] 1994 [cited 29 September 2008]. Available from the Internet: *http://www.stcdio.org/omf/marriage-ministry/7ReasonWhy.htm.*

17. Ibid.

18. Patrick F. Fagan. "Virgins Make the Best Valentines" National Review Online [online] 14 February 2007 [cited 29 September 2008]. Available from the Internet: *http://article.nationalreview.com/?q=MGNiODQ4YmEzMjc1ODc1YTYwNmIxM2Q5ZWZkZmE3YTM=#more.*

19. The National Longitudinal Survey of Adolescent Health, Wave II [online] 1996 [cited 29 September 2008]. Available from the Internet: *http://www.bls.gov/nls/.*

20. Robert E. Rector, Kirk A. Johnson, and Lauren R. Noyes, "Sexually Active Teenagers Are More Likely to Be Depressed and to Attempt Suicide," Heritage Center for Data Analysis [online] 200c [cited 29 September 2008]. Available from the Internet: *www.Heritage.org/research/abstinence/cda0304.crm.*

21. *Seventeen Magazine.* January 2003, 115.

22. Hanna Rosin. "Even Evangelical Teens Do It" [online] May 30, 2007 [cited 30 September 2008]. Available from the Internet: *http://www.slate.com/id/2167293/.*

23. Ibid.

24. Ibid.

25. Ibid.

26. Diana Jean Schemo. "Study Finds Mothers Unaware of Children's Sexual Activity" *The New York Times:* September 5, 2002. Available from the Internet: *http://www.nytimes.com/2002/09/05/national/05SEX.html*

27. Joan Jacobs Brumberg. *The Body Project: An Intimate History of American Girls* (New York: Vintage, 1998), 204.

28. Jane E. Brody. "Teenage Risks, and How to Avoid Them" in *The New York Times.* December 18, 2007. Available from the Internet: *http://www.nytimes.com/2007/12/18/health/18brod.html?_r=1&oref=slogin*

29. "Teen Girls Feel Pressured to Have Unwanted Sex." Archives of Pediatrics & Aoldescent Medicine, news release, June 5, 2006. Available from the Internet: *http://sexualhealth.e-healthsource.com/?p=news1&id=533103*

30. Barbara Dafoe Whitehead and Marline Pearson. "Making a Love Connection" from The National Campaign to Prevent Teen Pregnancy. [online] 2004 [cited 6 October 2008]. Available from the Internet: *http://peerta.acf.hhs.gov/uploadedFiles/Making_a_Love_Connection_FINAL.pdf*

31. If abortion is a part of your past, I highly recommend the study, *Surrendering the Secret* by Pat Layton.

32. Cynthia Dallard. "The Guttmacher Report on Public Policy." [online] August 2001 [cited 6 October 2008]. Available from the Internet: *http://www.guttmacher.org/pubs/tgr/04/4/gr040401.html*

33. National Campaign to Prevent Teen Pregnancy: With One Voice 2004: America's Adults and Teens Sound Off about Teen Pregnancy (December 2004)

34. Ibid.

35. Neil Howe and William Strauss. *Millenials Rising: The Next Great Generation.* (New York: Vintage, 2000), 200.

36. Diana Jean Schemo."Study Finds Mothers Unaware of Children's Sexual Activity" in *The New York Times* [online] 5 September 2002 [cited on 6 October 2008]. Available from the Internet: *http://www.nytimes.com/2002/09/05/national/05SEX.html*

37. Ibid.

38. Ibid.

39. Hanna Rosin. "Even Evangelical Teens Do It" [online] 30 May 2007 [cited 6 October 2008]. Available from the Internet: *http://www.slate.com/id/2167293/*

week four

1. "Happily Never After: New PTC Study Reveals TV Favors Non-Marital Sex" [online] 5 August 2008 [cited 8 October 2008]. Available from the Internet: *http://www.parentstv.org/PTC/news/release/2008/0805.asp*

2. Ibid.

3. Ibid.

4. Ibid.

5. Vanessa Mendenhall. "Are Young Evangelicals Leaning Left?" [online] 21 November 2006 [cited 8 October 2008]. Available from the Internet: *http://www.pbs.org/newshour/generation-next/demographic/religion3_11-21.html*

6. "Ellen DeGeneres: Portia de Rossi Will 'Cook and Clean' for Me" [online] 20 August 2008 [cited 9 October 2008]. Available from the Internet: *http://www.foxnews.com/story/0,2933,407121,00.html*

7. "Hallmark Begins Selling Same-Sex Wedding Cards" [online] 21 August 2008 [cited 9 October 2008]. Available from the Internet: *http://www.foxnews.com/story/0,2933,407761,00.html*

8. "Our Story" [online] n.d. [cited 9 October 2008]. Available from the Internet: *http://3rddate.com/ourstory.html*

9. "Sex Without Strings, Relationships Without Rings: Today's Young Singles Talk About Mating and Dating" A Publication of the National Marriage Project [online] 2000 [cited 9 October 2008]. Available from the Internet: *www.marriage.rutgers.edu*

10. Sharon Jayson and Anthony DeBarros. "Young adults delaying marriage" [online] 12 September 2007 [cited 9 October 2008]. Available from the Internet: *http:// www.usatoday.com/news/nation/2007-09-12-census-marriage_N.htm*

11. "Sex Without Strings, Relationships Without Rings"

12. David Popenoe and Barbara Dafoe Whitehead. "The Top Ten Myths of Marriage" [online] March 2002 [cited 9 October 2008]. Available from the Internet: *http://marriage.rutgers.edu/Publications/MythsMarriage.pdf*

13. "Seven Reasons Why Living Together Before Marriage is Not a Good Idea" [online] 3 January 2006 [cited 9 October 2008]. Available from the Internet: *http://www.stcdio.org/omf/marriage-ministry/7ReasonWhy.htm*

14. Judith Wallerstein, Julia Lewis, and Sharon Blakeslee. *The Unexpected Legacy of Divorce: A 25 Year Landmark Study* (New York: Hyperion, 2000), xxvii.

15. The National Marriage Project's Ten Things to Know Series, "The Top Ten Myths of Divorce" April 2001. David Popenoe and Barbara Dafoe Whitehead; Unpublished research by Linda J. Waite, cited in Linda J. Waite and Maggie Gallagher, The Case of Marriage (New York: Doubleday, 2000):148.

16. Ibid.

17. Ibid.

18. MD Anonymous. *Unprotected: A Campus Psychiatrist Reveals How Political Correctness in Her Profession Endangers Every Student* (New York: Sentinel, 2006), 123.

19. "Careers and babies: Fertility decline underscores dilemma" [online] 2 May 2002 [cited 9 October 2008]. Available from the Internet: *http://archives.cnn.com/2002/HEALTH/04/30/fertility.women/*

20. Sylvia Ann Hewlett. *Creating a Life: Professional Women and the Quest for Children* (New York: Hyperion, 2002), 116, 219.

21. Kate Johnson. "Oocyte Freezing: Insurance or False Security?" [online] February 2005 [cited 9 October 208]. Available from the Internet: *http://www.clinicalpsychiatrynews.com/article/PIIS0270664405707372/fulltext*

22. Ibid.

23. American Society for Reproductive Medicine, American Society for Reproductive medicine Guide for Patients, Infertility: An Overview (Birmingham, Ala.: American Society for Reproductive Medicine, 2003), 4.

24. Ibid.

25. A.D. Domar et al., "The Psychological Impact of Infertility: A Comparison with Patients with Other Medical Conditions," Journal of Psychosomatic Obstetrics and Gynecology 14 suppl. (1993), 45-52.

26. Zev Rosenwaks. "We Still Can't Stop the Biological Clock," *New York Times*, June 24, 2000. Available from the Internet: *http://query.nytimes.com/gst/fullpage.html?sec=health&res=940CE4DB1730F937A15755C0A9669C8B63.*

27. Sylvia Ann Hewlett, *Creating a Life: Professional Women and the Quest for Children* (New York: Hyperion, 2002), 217. Available from the Internet: *http://www.amazon.com/gp/reader/0786867663/ref=sib_dp_srch_pop?v=search-inside&keywords=217&go.x=0&go.y=0&go=Go%21#*

28. Helene Flournoy. "Young women picking marriage over careers" [online] 10 April 2007 [cited 15 October 2008]. Available from the Internet: *http://media.www.smudailycampus.com/media/storage/paper949/news/2007/04/10/News/Young.Women.Picking.Marriage.Over.Careers-2831756-page3.shtml*

29. Albert Mohler. "Choosing Motherhood Over Career? A Trend Among Young Women at Elite Universities" [online] 22 September 2005 [cited 16 October 2008]. Available from the Internet: *http://www.albertmohler.com/blog_read.php?id=291*

30. Ibid.

31. http://pewresearch.org/pubs/536/working-women; From: Fewer Mothers Prefer Full-time Work; From 1997 to 2007; July 12, 2007

32. Ibid.

week five

1. *http://en.wikipedia.org/wiki/Freak_dancing*

2. Melissa Marr, "Disney Reaches to the Crib to Extend Princess Magic," November 19, 2007, *www.online.wsj.com/public/article/SB119543097711697381.html.*

3. Generation Diva: Pampering could give little girls the wrong attitude; Lisa Nicita; The Arizona Republic; Jan. 15, 2008

4. Study: College Students More Narcissistic Than Ever; Tuesday, February 27, 2007; *http://www.foxnews.com/story/0,2933,254904,00.html*

5. Ibid.

6. Ibid.

7. For more information, go to *www.compassion.com.*

LEADER GUIDE

by Bethany McShurley

These suggestions will help you guide six sessions (75 to 90 minutes each) of *5 Conversations You Must Have with Your Daughter: The Bible Study*.

Every woman in your group will have a unique outlook, personal experiences, fears, and triumphs in her parenting story. So adapt these ideas to your group dynamic and join with God as He uses your group for His glory. Pray for the Lord's guidance in facilitating this study, and ask your prayer partners to do the same. Encourage participants to also enlist prayer partners.

Reserve your meeting place and secure a DVD player and television, session supplies such as notecards and pens, and adequate seating for the entire study. Consider soft music, candles, throw pillows, and fresh flowers to make your space feel relaxing and inviting. Enlist a volunteer to provide healthful snacks if desired.

If possible, arrange childcare during the study and promote this benefit in all of your advertising. Send postcards promoting the study and meeting times to all moms in your church whose daughters are preschool to college age. Consider use of the church promotional segment on DVD 1 (1:21).

Two weeks before your first meeting, post colorful flyers at church and possibly in the community to advertise. Be sure to have your event announced at church.

SESSION 1

Conversation 1: You are more than the sum of your parts.

In Advance

Obtain a variety of old fashion magazines.

Wrap a piece of jewelry in a grocery sack, and gift wrap an old dish towel or item of discarded clothing in an attractive box.

Welcome moms, introduce yourself, and ask each woman to share her name and the names/ages of her children. Ask: *What is your proudest parenting moment? What do you most hope to get out of this study?*

Play the conversation 1 opening segment (3:24) to highlight goals.

Encourage moms that the goal of the group is not to focus on imperfections but to grow in dependence on Christ and to bring up their daughters to be more like Jesus.

Displaying fashion magazines, ask: *In what ways do these represent culture's definition of beauty? In our time together we will better understand God's standards and help our girls do so. This will be accomplished through home features, Vicki's DVD teaching, discussing issues, and supporting each other.*

View

Continue the DVD with conversation 1 (3:25-25:11; viewer guide, p. 7). Ask two volunteers to open the packages you prepared. Comment: *Pretty packaging can be deceiving. Why must we look past the wrapping?*

Talk About

Ask moms to imagine they are planning a new magazine and addressing these content issues: (1) Whose face should grace the cover of your *God's Most Beautiful People* magazine? Why? (2) Brainstorm ideas for articles and visual images you would use to sell this idea: Inner beauty is more important than physical attractiveness.

• *Option:* See the viewer guide on page 7 for additional discussion questions.

Encourage women to skim pages 1-36 in their books. Acquaint them with the interactive elements on pages 4-5. Comment: *The Lord offers hope and help, both for us and for our daughters. This Bible study group experience will help us discover His truths and learn how to apply them.*

Support and Pray

Ask moms to share names and phone numbers/e-mail addresses to stay in touch. Say: *One of our best resources as mothers is other mothers who love the Lord.*

Close in prayer, asking God to touch each mom's heart with a fresh love for her daughter and renewed commitment to be the best mom she can with the Lord's help.

Remind the group to complete the week 1 home study before the next group meeting.

SESSION 2

Conversation 2: Don't be in such a hurry to grow up.

In Advance

Gather items that represent growing-up milestones for girls: earrings, deodorant, high heels, a bra, lipstick, car keys, a razor, a poster or framed picture of a teenage guy, a diary, and a cell phone.

Week 1 Review

Sessions 2-6 have options to review each previous week's home study. Choose your own questions from the workbook; show bonus footage; or select an option from among the following (watch your time!):

• Do you recall family members making statements to you about your weight or the need to stay in shape? How old were you, what was the statement, who made it, and how did you feel? How does it impact the message you send your daughter?

• Ask: *What does this quote by Ralph Waldo Emerson mean to you after week 1?* "Though we travel the world over to find the beautiful, we must carry it with us or we find it not."

• Ask volunteers to share how God's definition of true beauty influenced their interactions with their daughters and perceptions of themselves this week.

View

Play DVD conversation 2 (20:54; viewer guide, p. 37). Then group moms in pairs, giving each twosome a growing-up item.

Ask pairs to discuss: (1) Why is the item crucial (or not) to growing up? (2) How might we know when our girls are ready for this milestone? (3) How has the need/age changed since we were girls? After 10 minutes call for reports. Affirm that moms will discover more on this topic next week.

Talk About

Ask the group to share times when women in their lives lovingly led them to make wise growing-up choices.

Options: Use a question from the viewer guide (p. 37) or select a Meet Our Moms bonus response to the question *Do you struggle to find a balance when it comes to saying yes, no, or wait?*

Briefly discuss the importance of not passing judgment on parenting choices of other Christian moms—and of mentoring and praying for each other instead.

Support and Pray

Close: *Take one notecard for each of your daughters, writing their first and middle names. Pass cards to your left. Pray over the names you receive— that God would help girls grow into young women who are pleasing to Him.*

SESSION 3
Conversation 3: Sex is great and worth the wait.

Pray, thanking God for your group and asking His guidance in teaching daughters about His perfect plan for their lives.

Week 2 Review

- If a conversation was initiated based on pages 46-49, how did it go?
- Respond to "The Friendship Factor" (day 4). How can you help your daughter build positive friendships and avoid negative ones?

Ask volunteers to describe their first romantic crush or the first time they were interested in a boy. What was his name? How old were they?

Encourage moms to share advice their mothers offered regarding boy/girl relationships.

View

Overview conversation 3 with Vicki's DVD teaching (30:23; viewer guide, p. 75).

Talk About

Ask a volunteer to play the role of a virgin bride at her bridal shower. Moms are shower guests and must give the bride advice about her honeymoon night. Of course, keep things clean, but encourage both serious and funny responses. Insist that the "bride" maintain eye contact with speakers. *Option:* Give a small prize for the "best" advice. Point out to the group: *Having "the talk" is not as daunting as it may seem.*

What qualifies a Christian mom as the best person to talk to her daughter about sex? Write group responses on a visual.

Ask: *What are society's consistent messages about sex and sensuality?* Discuss the value of having a form of "the talk" on a consistent basis and how the week 3 home study will help moms begin to do so.

Support and Pray

Distribute notecards. Ask mothers to write down what they consider the greatest benefit of saving sex for marriage (and/or their greatest fear to having this conversation).

Pray that God will give each mom confidence to hold ongoing communication with her daughter about maintaining purity. Ask for special blessing and guidance for any moms whose girls are in rebellion.

SESSION 4

Conversation 4: It's OK to dream about marriage and motherhood.

Ask: *What do you most enjoy about being a wife or mom?* Thank God for the privilege of serving Him through families.

Week 3 Review

- What cultural messages about sex caught your attention last week?
- What most shocked/surprised you about conversation 3? (Also see Meet Our Moms.)

View

Continue with DVD conversation 4 (18:54; viewer guide, p. 107).

Talk About

"And they lived happily ever after" concludes many fairy-tale love stories. *As a group, define a traditional "happily ever after" scenario.* After responses, assure: *If you have experienced brokenness and are rearing children in the midst of a painful breakup, know that God loves you, is willing to forgive, and wants you to move on in victory.*

Show a visual labeled "Super Woman" and assign: *List things a woman should be or do to gain mainstream approval. Use another color to list qualities God desires for Christians. Overlap is OK.*

Ask: *What can we do to help our girls pursue godly life goals over worldly expectations that contradict His plan?*

Comment: *Culture equates motherhood with negatives.* Encourage moms to shout positives to counter each of these "down sides": Weight gain, little free time, sleeplessness, worn hands, tired wardrobe, less spending money.

Support and Pray

Spend time praying for each other's marriages and/or families.

SESSION 5

Conversation 5: Girls gone wild are a dime a dozen—dare to be virtuous.

Ask moms to share ways their attitude toward their role is evolving, and encourage them to stay the course.

Week 4 Review

- What changes are occurring in your interactions with your girl(s)?

- Share one point in your script to help your daughter reconcile the divorce with God's intent for marriage.

View

Play the DVD with Vicki's teaching of conversation 5 (24:42; viewer guide, p. 137).

Talk About

Discuss the value of a good reputation. How does reputation affect friendships? business? family? explain. Vicki comments that "bad is the new good." Ask: *What evidence of her statement do we see all around us?*

What tools can we use and whom can we enlist to help us rear our girls for Christ? To what safeguards and examples can we expose our daughters that would counter the bad-girl image culture supports? Discuss responses.

Support and Pray

Close, asking God to help each mom view her life through His eyes—and to do whatever is necessary to help lead her daughter to Christ or strengthen her walk with Him.

SESSION 6

Give each mother a votive as a reminder of this experience. Explain: *In a morally dark world, Christians can shine with the light of Christ. Believing moms can light the way to godliness for their girls as they daily lean on the Lord for strength.*

Week 5 Review

- Indicate a service opportunity you may do with your daughter (day 3).
- Share the verse you used as a personal prayer for your daughter (p. 163).

Hand out cards, assuring each mom she won't be asked to share what she writes. Ask the group to jot down a prayer for each daughter and to hold onto prayers as they watch the video.

View and Talk About

Conclude video teaching with "The Final Charge" (DVD, 16:52; viewer guide, p. 165). Observe: *Protecting and maturing our girls is a team effort; we must rely on God for help. What can we do to make sure we are aligning ourselves with His desires for our lives and families?* Affirm responses, especially the role of prayer.

Support and Pray

Ask moms to silently pray over the requests they wrote earlier. Then encourage them to gather in groups of 2-4, praying for strength and guidance in their journeys and for God's protection and intervention in their daughters' lives.

Remind moms to keep in touch with one another. Encourage them to set up recurring mom-daughter dates to stay engaged.

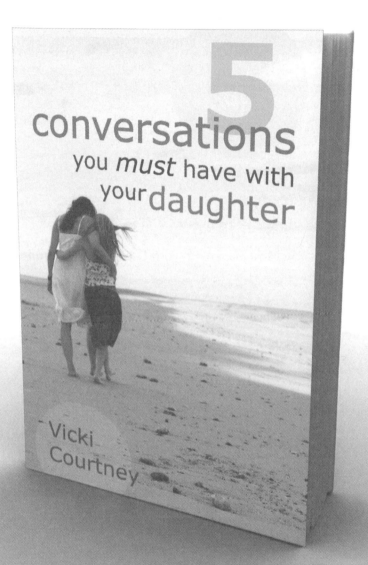

104296

CHRISTIAN GROWTH STUDY PLAN

Christian Growth Study Plan resources are available for course credit for personal growth and church leadership training.

Courses are designed as plans for personal spiritual growth and for training current and future church leaders. To receive credit, complete the book, material, or activity. Respond to the learning activities or attend group sessions, when applicable, and show your work to your pastor, staff member, or church leader. Then go to *www.lifeway.com/CGSP*, or call the toll-free number for instructions for receiving credit and your certificate of completion.

For information about studies in the Christian Growth Study Plan, refer to the current catalog online at the CGSP Web address. This program and certificate are free LifeWay services to you.

CONTACT INFORMATION:
Christian Growth Study Plan
One LifeWay Plaza, MSN 117
Nashville, TN 37234
Toll free 1-800-968-5519
Fax 1-615-251-5067
Email: cgspnet@lifeway.com
www.lifeway.com/CGSP
Order resources: 800-458-2772

5 Conversations You Must Have with Your Daughter: The Bible Study

Subject Area: Personal Life. Course Number: CG-1439

PARTICIPANT INFORMATION

Social Security Number (USA ONLY-optional)

Personal CGSP Number*

Date of Birth (MONTH, DAY, YEAR)

Name (First, Middle, Last)

Home Phone

Address (Street, Route, or P.O. Box)

City, State, or Province

Zip/Postal Code

Email Address for CGSP use

Please check appropriate box: ❑ Resource purchased by church ❑ Resource purchased by self ❑ Other

CHURCH INFORMATION

Church Name

Address (Street, Route, or P.O. Box)

City, State, or Province

Zip/Postal Code

CHANGE REQUEST ONLY

☐ Former Name

☐ Former Address — City, State, or Province — Zip/Postal Code

☐ Former Church — City, State, or Province — Zip/Postal Code

Signature of Pastor, Conference Leader, or Ot

Date

*New participants are requested but not required ... for the first time.
Thereafter, only one ID# is required. **Mail to: Ch** ... -5067.

Revised 4-05